HONESTLY,
I'm Struggling

To order additional copies of *Honestly, I'm Struggling,*
by Heather Bohlender,
call **1-800-765-6955.**

Visit us at **www.reviewandherald.com**
for information on other Review and Herald® products.

HONESTLY,
I'm Struggling

Living Beyond the Student Missionary Cliché

Heather Bohlender

WITH Chris Blake

REVIEW AND HERALD® PUBLISHING ASSOCIATION
Since 1861 | www.reviewandherald.com

Published by Review and Herald® Publishing Association, Hagerstown, MD 21741-1119

Review and Herald® titles may be purchased in bulk for educational, business, fund-raising, or sales promotional use. For information, e-mail SpecialMarkets@reviewandherald.com.

The Review and Herald® Publishing Association publishes biblically based materials for spiritual, physical, and mental growth and Christian discipleship.

The author assumes full responsibility for the accuracy of all facts and quotations as cited in this book.

Unless otherwise noted, texts are from *The Message.* Copyright © 1993, 1994, 1995, 1996, 2000, 2002. Used by permission of NavPress Publishing Group.

This book was
Edited by Kalie Kelch
Copyedited by James Hoffer
Cover designed by Trent Truman
Interior designed by Tina M. Ivany
Typeset: Bembo 11/14

PRINTED IN U.S.A.

14 13 12 11 10   5 4 3 2 1

Library of Congress Cataloging-in-Publication Data

Bohlender, Heather, 1987–
  Honestly, I'm struggling : living beyond the student missionary cliché / Heather Bohlender; with Chris Blake.
      p. cm.
1. Bohlender, Heather, 1987– 2. Missionaries—Cambodia—Biography. 3. Seventh-Day Adventists—Cambodia—Biography. I. Blake, Chris, 1951– II. Title.
  BV3306.2.B64A3 2010
  266'.6732596092—dc22
  [B]
                              2009039417

ISBN 978-0-8280-2449-5

To my students in Cambodia

You taught me lessons I never could have learned in a college textbook. You opened my eyes to a new world and a new way of living.

This book is the product of the blogs I wrote about my experience in Cambodia.

Living halfway around the world from home was hard. Sometimes I cried, and sometimes I wanted to go home. Please know that as difficult as it was to be separated from my friends and family, you, my students, made it easier for me every day, and you are the reason I stayed.

The names in this book have been changed. I value our friendships and wouldn't expose that to anyone. You shared deep parts of yourselves that I want to remember forever. So don't look for your name, because they are all mixed up. The Ratana I write about may not be the Ratana you're thinking about. Now they are just characters in a great story, a story you helped me write, a story you are still writing.

This book is for you.

Thank you,
Ms. Bo

ACKNOWLEDGMENTS

To Cambodia and to my students, thank you for the lessons you taught me that I'll never forget. I came to teach, but I learned so much more.

To Tim and Fay Scott, my parents in Cambodia, I wouldn't have survived the year without your love, patience, and guidance. Thanks for listening and getting me through. Now you're stuck with me forever.

To Polly, my tough, insightful, and brave friend, you amaze me. Thanks for the prayers. I'm still looking forward to our road trip, someday.

To Ashley and Ben, two of the wisest, most wonderful human beings on planet earth, I love you both. Thanks for helping me feel safe, understood, and a little less crazy.

To Mom and Dad, thanks, first of all, for the good genes, but more importantly, thank you for loving me and never giving up on me when I've given you plenty of reasons to.

To Pastor Rich Carlson, thanks for flying all the way to Cambodia to get me started and for your support and prayers every step of the way. Thank you for your friendship, guidance, and peace of mind.

To Mr. Blake, thank you for your patience, insight, and wisdom. I'm grateful. Thanks for being a huge part of the journey and helping me find my way through the writing of this book. Thank you for your excellent editing skills that have turned my third-grade ramblings into an eloquent, book-worthy masterpiece.

I owe a huge, monstrous thank you to everyone that I can't possibly mention right here, right now. To my counselors, friends, family, and other beautiful people who have carried/supported me through this journey, thank you. Also for the letters, e-mail messages, care packages, and prayers, your graciousness will never be forgotten.

Spirit, for the breath in my body and for waking me up today, thank you is not enough—but thank You. I'm up for the journey. I'm along for the ride. Lead me on.

Contents

FORWARD

Wow! That's different!

Those words blew through my mind when I first read Heather Bohlender's journal blogs from Cambodia.

So did *honest, courageous, disturbing, insightful, inspiring.*

Soon Heather and I began discussing possibilities of turning her blog entries into a book aimed at young adults. Actually, a book aimed at anybody who has been wrestling with purpose, wracked by loneliness, and wrecked on the world's heartbreaking injustices.

Although this is Heather's tale, it's also the story of all of us who have ever felt "othered" and had to weather judgmental finger-pointing—particularly from the one we can't seem to get away from. Ourselves.

In a culture cracked like an overripe melon, we witness what happens when fear dominates. In the whirling vortex of a city intersection. In a sweaty classroom. In the crippling grip of an eating disorder. In Cambodia, where fear holds sway through haunting memories of recent atrocities.

Within this stunningly foreign land, Heather moves from trying to change the world to trying to change her tiny ripple—every person she comes in contact with. She moves from doing her best to doing her balanced best.

True followers of Jesus are those who creatively and honestly battle, not the seductive war against sinless living but the good fight of faith. Doing justly. Loving mercy. Walking humbly with our God. We don't merely sweep the house clean; we fill every space with gracious goodness. We discover the holiest approach to life is unvarnished truth.

So how do we endure the slings and arrows of outrageous fortune?

We take courage. Keep our mind and eyes open. Go forward with defiant optimism. Experience freedom and hope.

We live in peace, by grace, for love, with joy.

This story is indeed different, but I'll take that over a stereotypical, feel-good fable any day.

—Chris Blake
Associate Professor of English and Communication
Union College

CHAPTER 1

Down and Out

"I can be changed by what happens to me. I refuse to be reduced by it."
—*Maya Angelou*

What in the world am I doing here?

Rain drenches me as I sit in the middle of a busy Cambodian street. It is difficult to breathe with the dense water pouring over my head. Six inches of muddy, trashy liquid sweeps past me, a pathetic, hurting island in the midst of chaos.

Minutes before, a car hit me, and now I am sitting in the street in a daze. I had been riding my bike around town running some errands when, at my last stop, the storm began. A Khmer woman, face ravaged by acid burns, talked excitedly to me as I walked out the door. "Srey saat [*Beautiful*]," she squealed in my direction as I turned to go. Her smiling face was covered in red, painful-looking blisters that would always look that way.

She handed me a plastic poncho. I was going to need it. "Bongsrey! Akoon [*Thank you, sister*]."

Several inches of water had already accumulated on the eternally busy streets. I tightened the hood of the poncho around my face until a narrow oval remained to see through. Immediately, I was soaked. Not much escapes these tropical downpours.

Just as I was nearing home, a car sped from behind me, grazing my left hip. I tried to correct myself, but the unexpected force sent me tumbling. Screaming, I fell hard to the ground. A sharp pain shot through my left shoulder. The car kept going, and so did the rest of the traffic, splashing water on me from their passing tires. The traffic never paused, not even for a second.

As I sit in the dirty water with my bike piled on top of me, I want to cry. But as the thought emerges, I look up to see several Cambodian men pointing and laughing at me.

So, instead, I slowly stand up and assess the damage: no broken bones. However, my legs and the palms of my hands are thrashed and bleeding, and my favorite sandals are broken. With the poncho plastered to my wet body, I stoop to pick up my bike. Grabbing the twisted handlebars, I ride home.

It could've been much worse I realize later as I treat my wounds, trying to recall what happened. But those thoughts don't console me, because a trend seems to be developing in my life, one of problems and trials. I can't help wondering how many more hits I can take.

Since landing in Cambodia, the questions never cease. *Why does this have to hurt so much? What am I turning into? Why can't I understand these people? God, are You there?*

Tonight is no different. Like so many other nights, one primary thought remains: *What in the world am I doing here?*

CHAPTER 2

The Idea

"Trust God from the bottom of your heart; don't try to figure out everything on your own. Listen for God's voice in everything you do, everywhere you go."
—*Proverbs 3:5, 6*

Months earlier, flying to Cambodia seemed like a no-brainer. Ever since childhood I had listened to missionaries tell their breathless stories in church, and I always thought, *Someday, I'm going to do that.*

During the second semester of my freshman year at Union College, I read an e-mail from Pastor Rich, the school chaplain, about the need for a student missionary. So, I hopped on it. At the time I wasn't dating anyone and hadn't picked a major, so I felt I should go before I came up with a lame excuse not to.

For the next month I pursued the opportunity, barely making time to call my parents to say, "So what do you think about your little girl being a missionary?" Everything about the choice just seemed right—terrifying, but right. I informed friends and family that I wouldn't be in the U.S. the next year. I would be in Cambodia.

I knew there was a big world "out there." Easy as it was to get wrapped up in the media, popularity, and drama in America, I sensed there was something more.

Eager for adventure, I wanted to give God an entire year of my life to do with me what He pleased. I wanted to run away with God. I didn't care where. (For the record, I am not the super-Christian type who has always been close to God.) So I figured giving Him free reign was the best way to get to know Him for myself.

The weeks before my flight left me excited but anxious. I spent extra time with the people I loved, fully aware that anything could happen while I was gone. My grandparents weren't getting any younger. I understood that I would miss out on a year with family and friends. I had to prepare myself for big changes when I returned. Of course, my family was also preparing for the time apart.

"You are going to come back a different person," they said. "We will e-mail you all the time. We'll pray for you."

At the time I gave their prayers little thought.

"Promise you won't have any fun while I'm gone, OK? No pregnancies, no marriages. Just put your lives on hold for me, all right?" I begged.

Smiling, family and friends agreed: no fun till I got back.

I was scheduled to leave on August 22. I would be gone until July, more than 10 months later. I cried as I lugged the last bag out of my bedroom. I cried as I called my sister on the way to the airport.

"Please, please don't forget about me while I'm in Cambodia," I sobbed into the cell phone.

I cried as I left my parents at security. I wasn't scared for my safety so much as receiving a dreaded phone call about theirs. I sobbed as I walked toward my gate.

Then, I forced myself into a serious mental shift. *It's time. Let's go, chica.*

I had to face the new reality staring me in the face. Next stop, Cambodia. I boarded the plane and flew off to unknown adventures.

CHAPTER 3

City I'll Call Home

"The same thing gets said about us when we embrace and believe the One who brought Jesus to life when the conditions were equally hopeless. The sacrificed Jesus made us fit for God, set us right with God."
—Romans 4:24, 25

Well, here I sit. I made it to Cambodia.

I'm actually surprised to be here. "Talking" about going and actually "going" to Cambodia are vastly different. However surreal, it's true. I am here, touching Cambodian soil with my own feet, smelling Cambodian air with my own nose. Going back is not an option.

It has been scary traveling around the world alone, and I am already beginning to second-guess my decision to come. *Why did you ever think this was a good idea? Heather, you idiot.*

At the airport my thoughts are interrupted as I meet two other student missionaries, Liz and Trina, and our hosts, Tim and Fay Scott. Liz and Trina are from Walla Walla College, and they chat excitedly about what we'll be experiencing in Cambodia. Tim and Fay work at the school where we'll be teaching. Tim, the school superintendent, is tall and slim. Fay, the librarian and student missionary "mom," is shorter with curly, brown hair. Missionary veterans who have served overseas for nearly 20 years, both smile warmly, and I immediately feel at ease. Fay envelopes me in a bear hug, which is surprisingly affectionate for our first five seconds together.

"It's so wonderful to finally meet you!" she says, beaming. "We are going to get you all settled in here. How was your flight?"

"Um, good I guess." *Is my disorientation obvious?*

We gather our luggage and pile into a beat-up van. A bucket seat pulls down for me to sit on, which is a tight squeeze. Sweat starts trickling down my back. We sit close enough to rub each other's skin. Intense heat, dust, and exhaust pour into the van's open windows.

"Well, this is Cambodia," Fay chirps as we head into the hustling streets. "It may all seem a bit overwhelming, but you'll get used to it."

Tim drives on as Fay chats like an excited tour guide.

The sun shines like a spotlight on my face. In spite of the intense light, my eyes are open wide as a child's, struggling to take it all in. Constantly merging traffic, honking horns, and near-accidents appear at every turn. Everyone believes they have the right-of-way. If we actually sit at the red light and wait for the green light, we may never move. Ever.

Locals driving moped-style bikes they call motos whiz about and congest the teeming roads. No one wears a helmet. That would imply sanity.

We drop our bags off at the Adventist mission and take a brief tour of Phnom Penh, the capital of Cambodia. Busy, noisy open-air markets dominate every corner of the city. Bright orange peppers, mini-sized watermelons, bananas, and deep purple eggplants lay on wooden tables or dirt-covered floors. Congested with people, dogs, heavy humidity, and yelling vendors, there is so much to take in as we explore the city. However foreign it seems, Phnom Penh is home for the next 10 months.

CHAPTER 4

So This Is Life

"Do for God what you said you'd do—he is, after all, your God. . . .
Nobody gets by with anything, no one plays fast and loose with him."
—Psalm 76:11, 12

Wide awake at 6:30 a.m. Where am I? Staring up at the strange ceiling, struggling to get my bearings, it suddenly dawns on me, I'm in Cambodia.

After only a short time in Cambodia, I feel like my world is spinning. There are new customs to learn—like always taking your shoes off when entering a church or a person's house—and a new language to try to understand. Khmer is the language, and it sounds like a nasally whine—which is even more annoying when you can't understand a word.

Nearly everyone wears a surgical mask to cover their nose and mouth when they are out on the street. Dirt and pollution are constantly present and painful to breathe in. Another cultural difference I must adjust to is that men are incredibly affectionate, holding hands and rubbing each other's backs. It is obvious that Cambodians lack any personal bubble. They stand and walk far too close to me. It makes me nervous. In Cambodia it is perfectly acceptable to stare at someone who looks different, and since I look different, I am a constant target for their penetrating eyes.

Thoughts about my new surroundings swirl in my head as I walk to church my first Sabbath in Cambodia. All too quickly, I realize I'm the main attraction. *Step right up! See the pale American! Isn't it amazing?* Everyone watches as I make my way to the only open seat in the front row. The service is completely in Khmer: song service, testimonies, sermon. I don't get a whole lot out of it.

Honestly, I am trying so hard to live in the moment and enjoy the experience for what it is, but I can't help thinking, *This is not what I expected.*

The feeling of absolute isolation is almost indescribable. It's awful. I don't know anyone here. While Liz and Trina have also come from the U.S., they were friends before coming, so they have each other for support. We don't have much in common other than geographic location.

I'm not so sure I'm strong enough for this; I wish I were the kind of person who could just put emotions aside. But, as the outsider, I am lonely. I crave real relationships, and I don't see anyone else here who can even speak English. I desperately desire a connection with someone, anyone who would make this more bearable. I realize that even if I could call home, everyone is asleep right now. I won't lie; if someone offered me a ticket home right now, I would take it.

Overwhelmed with my thoughts, I struggle to breathe. Although I'm surrounded by fellow believers in the presence of God, I feel like I'm drowning.

My mind keeps whirling about my current situation. Although I long for companionship, I also need time alone, something else that is not possible here. My apartment is made for one person, but we are squeezing in three. The front room harbors a stove, a refrigerator, and a couch. Our bedroom is just wide enough for a three-tiered bunk bed.

The bathroom is crazy cramped. It's smaller than my closet at home. I can sit on the toilet, take a shower, and brush my teeth all at the same time, though I don't think I'll try. The shower sprays directly on the toilet. The "space" we share is very claustrophobic. Time alone is a joke. I fluctuate from needing time alone to get a grasp on my environment, to needing at least one person to talk to, a friend, community. I can hardly think straight.

If only I could exercise and pray to clear my head and find peace. But this doesn't seem to be an option. Being outside alone isn't safe, and being inside the apartment is crowded. If it is any indication about the safety in our area, the church compound features a guard, strict security, 10-foot walls, and three locks to open before I reach my apartment.

The Internet shop three hundred yards from the compound is not safe to walk to at night, even with men, even in a group. Gang rapes and robberies are common in the area. The police don't do anything unless you bribe them. Being a blondish American, I can't hide. Everyone has something to say to me.

"Hello, pretty lady. Where you come from? You want to come home with me?"

My wandering mind momentarily stops as the church service comes to a close. I leave the building and take a fresh look at my surroundings. Outside the compound I see majestic mansions dotting the streets, much as one would see in Beverly Hills, California. Right next to them sits a pathetic shack. I see a family on the side of the road. The husband and wife run a shop selling dead pigs hanging from hooks. Two naked children play in the street puddles, which are littered with floating dirty diapers. Their family's shack consists of a metal sheet for a roof and is filled with wet, moldy mattresses, trash, and a stray dog.

This scene makes me realize that it's hard to complain about my situation when I could be living like my new neighbors every day.

One day down.

CHAPTER 5

A Better Teacher

I'm sure now I'll see God's goodness in the exuberant earth. Stay with God!
Take heart. Don't quit. I'll say it again: Stay with God."
—*Psalm 27:13, 14*

Cambodia Adventist School is a compound of thatched walls stuck to-gether to form twelve classrooms. Dirty tile floors and broken desks fill each room. Each class sports large square holes cut out of the walls to make windows. Metal hooks suspend large panels that serve as window flaps, which are opened and closed at the start and end of each day.

Tears ambush my eyes as I try to fight them off. *This is where I am supposed to teach?*

A separate concrete building houses about forty dormitory students in two large rooms, one for boys, one for girls. Each room contains bunk beds without mattresses. A small kitchen sits between the girls' and boys' side.

The second floor features the office, bathrooms, and library/computer lab. Outside is a shaded picnic area. Surrounding the campus stands a 10-foot wall with a guard at the gate. While the average temperature in Phnom Penh is 90 degrees, we have no air conditioning and only come-and-go electricity.

Forty staff members work at Cambodia Adventist School or CAS for short. This year we expect about 400 students. I thought I was going to teach fourth grade, but plans have changed. I may be teaching seventh-grade read-ing, eighth-grade geography, and tenth- and eleventh-grade English. I may also be teaching drama and Bible and helping in kindergarten.

At teacher orientation a CAS teacher says, "Being American already makes you a good teacher."

"I don't believe that! Why am I a better teacher?" I inquire, utterly con-fused. "I've never taught a day in my life. I have no idea what I'm doing."

She explains, "You've been taught in the United States. The level of education is higher. So, even being an American student means you might be the best teacher these kids ever have."

Many tired people make up the staff at CAS. Nearly 85 percent of the staff is Khmer, and English is, of course, their second language. Even though this is allegedly an English-speaking school, they continue to speak Khmer. The handbook says: speak English, do not chew gum, turn off your cell phones, and wear a tie, but rarely are all of the rules enforced. There is much confusion and little consistency.

Just thinking about being left alone with thirty Khmer children makes my heart race like a greyhound. And apparently I am supposed to teach them stuff too. *What can I teach them? I'm not a teacher. I'm a volunteer.* Inadequacy floods my thoughts as I sit in teacher orientation thinking, *The principal knows I'm not actually a teacher, right?*

Fay and Tim Scott teach at CAS and live on the compound. Fay is genuine and kind and actually shows concern. Tim is warm and a good leader. If yesterday's encounter with Fay is any indication, I think she will be the best support for me while I am here.

It all happened when I stopped by her house on my way back from talking to my mom on the phone. "How was the Internet connection?" she asked me.

"Oh, it was fine, if she could understand me through my sobbing."

Fay looked surprised at my honesty, but genuine concern showed on her face, and she asked if I was OK. Crying again, I unloaded on her. "I'm struggling. I can't imagine living and working here."

Fay is a veteran missionary, so after I ran out of things to say, I shut up and listened.

"Tim and I have been living overseas in different countries for 20 years now. You have been here for three days. Haven't you ever struggled to adjust to anything else in your life?"

I think back across my life. Of course I've struggled. It's a distant memory now, but yeah, I cried during my first few weeks of my freshman year at college. It was hard to meet people and fit in, even when they were speaking my language.

I've done the college thing. Now, I suppose I'm doing the Cambodia thing. I pick myself up and head back to my room ready to tackle the challenge before me.

Unfortunately, reality is a beast. As I lie on my bed, I can't fall asleep in the stifling heat. *How do people live this way? How am I supposed to teach?*

Finally, I drift off into a restless sleep, dreaming about my family and friends erasing me from photos and putting in new people they like better.

I am not sleeping well, and with each passing day it isn't getting any easier. Every time I check my e-mail, I cry. I miss the community I have back at home, the one that I have obviously taken for granted for so long. At the Internet shop closest to my apartment, the owner always looks at me sadly. I'm sure he is thinking, *Why does this girl keep coming here and doing this to herself?*

On my way to school I swing by the Internet shop to gain encouragement to get through the day. My inbox swims in e-mail messages titled "Praying for You" and "We Love You." I get it. I realize that there are many, many prayers coming from America, but unfortunately, I have very little trust on my part.

Leaving the shop, I start praying as I ride to school on my bike. All day I chant to myself, "We can do this. Just get me through the next five minutes. We can do this. God, help me. Please help me through this." All day.

It isn't like God hasn't been there all along, but I haven't been asking for His help. I never could have prepared myself for all of this. Never.

After reading some more e-mails from home, I catch my breath a little bit. Living here is overwhelming and stressful, but I smiled yesterday. I think I laughed. I'm more keenly aware of God's presence. Of course, He was always there; I just wasn't noticing. I'm beginning to believe that the shock of Cambodia doesn't have to dominate me.

I start to see things differently. I notice a Cambodian teacher when she reaches for my hand while talking to me. Another teacher from Burma touches my arm. I didn't realize how much I was craving physical contact, but this new connection feels good.

I am crying less. I am taking deeper breaths. I am trying to connect more with God. I am learning and living a great adventure for my heavenly Father. I am, as Abraham described himself, a stranger in a strange land. *God, get me through.*

CHAPTER 6

"I Am Ms. Bo"

"Every day is a new beginning. Treat it that way. Stay away from what might have been, and look at what can be."
—*Marsha Petrie Sue*

Four hundred red and white uniformed students flood the gates like an approaching army. My eyes shift nervously left to right, scanning the enemy. Sweat pours from every possible gland on my body. My entire body tenses as I fear the worst. Can I convince them that I know what I am doing?

Half walking, half stumbling, I trudge up to them. It is hard to keep my stern posture when some members of the opposing army are three feet tall and sport pigtails. Regardless, I recognize their plot to "get" me. As I line up with my eighth grade class, they sing Cambodia's national anthem, and I lead them to our classroom.

I am supposed to be a teacher, right? I am Ms. Bo. There's no turning back now.

"Good morning, eighth graders!" I beam at them.

They frown and cross their arms.

"I am so happy to have each of you in this class. My name is Ms. Bo. I am from the United States."

They continue looking unimpressed and a little confused. Can they understand what I am saying?

I read a worship thought and pray with the less-than-thrilled eighth graders who will be my homeroom students all year long. After my introduction, which seemed about as exciting to them as watching fishing on television, I head for the rest of my classes. Mostly, I'll be teaching high school students, which I am grateful for. They appear friendly, well-mannered, and I think they understand what I am saying.

Taking roll in my first English class, I sigh heavily just trying to pronounce the names. "Lim? Prom? Pen?" Not a sound. "Umm, am I saying any of these names correctly?"

Snickers rise from students around the room. Finally, a kind soul pipes up. "You are only reading part of their names. See, here we write our family name first, then after that, the name we answer to."

"Oh, so you write your last names first?"

"No, we write our first names first," they correct me.

"But you just said your last names . . . oh, your *family* name! In America I'm used to 'first' and 'last' names. OK, if I was writing my name the way Cambodians do, I'd be 'Bohlender Heather,' right?"

They grin and a few roll their eyes at my small accomplishment that took the first 15 minutes of class.

My high school students' English is poor, but it is far better than the younger kids. Throughout the day I catch them fingering my light, curly hair and comparing their deep brown skin tones to my white, freckled skin.

I am trying to be firm but kind. I don't want to get walked all over this year. I introduce myself to them, clearly state my rules and expectations, and introduce a few subjects we'll be covering during the year. Some might call it teaching. I call it winging it. I really don't know what I'm doing.

My positive thoughts about the high school students are brought back to reality, when Fay tells me later, "It won't last. They will get used to the fact that you are white and pretty, and then they will really start pushing your buttons."

She is probably right. The shock factor that I am an American will wear off. Then I will be left with who knows what.

Little do I know that the most challenging part of my day is still ahead of me, dealing with the seventh graders. These kiddos must all compare notes on how to anger and frustrate the teachers. Maybe they hold powwows outside the gate before school each day.

I imagine it goes something like this: "OK, you run around the class yelling, then I'll steal her backpack, and you guys just start hitting each other. Got it? Go!"

If any class is going to get to me, it will be these kids. Pushing water upstream would be easier than keeping them on task. They don't really come to school to learn. They come to make teachers cry and then go play with their friends.

Yet, all in all, I feel fairly confident after my first-ever day of teaching. I just hope it is all downhill from here. My jumbled early morning thoughts— *These kids won't attack you. Now, say something intelligent. Are they still watching? Say something; say anything! You dork. God, get me through.*—are replaced with the reality that I made it.

My mind continues to process the day. I wonder, do I notice God only in the huge, miraculous answers to prayer and overlook the fact that, somehow, I am still breathing? Yes.

I prayed for strength to make it through today, and I did. How is that not an answer to prayer? I give myself way too much credit. *Thank you, Jesus. Thank you that I am alive. Thank you for helping me make it through my day.*

As I walk home from school, it starts to rain. It seems that the rain dumps predictably at 3:00 p.m. every day. Most of the roads are dirt and full of potholes. Wading in my flip-flops through the brown water, which is full of food wrappers and garbage, I actually chuckle as the reality sets in: I am shuffling through germ-infested water in soggy flip-flops on my way "home" to my too-tiny apartment in Cambodia after a long day at school. Ha.

I mutter a few "Ughs" and "Ewws" before I make it, soaking wet, back to my apartment. I'm wet and tired, but I have a prayer in my heart: *Dear God, I am still breathing. Thank You that I am still breathing.*

CHAPTER 7

Different

There's more to come: We continue to shout our praise even when we're hemmed in with troubles, because we know how troubles can develop passionate patience in us, and how that patience in turn forges the tempered steel of virtue, keeping us alert for whatever God will do next."
—Romans 5:3, 4

Teaching in Cambodia is just. . . different.

Skirts and flip-flops will be my uniform all year. My trusty steed is a bright red mountain bike that will never see a mountain, but it helps me feel braver on the streets. I pull on my headphones. On my way to school, I pass palaces with marble tile, uniformed guards, and manicured green landscaping. I also ride by shacks with weary poor people sitting out front. They stare unashamed at me as I nervously navigate my way around the huge potholes of reddish water.

School may not start for an hour, but half the students are already waiting for us.

"Why are you here so early?" I ask.

"We have nowhere else to go," they answer matter-of-factly, and return to their conversations I can't understand.

I open the door to my classroom: dusty tile floors, 27 mostly broken wooden desks, a whiteboard, thatched walls and roof.

It's only 7:00 a.m. and already I am sweating more than a step-aerobics instructor working out in a sauna.

Each morning we line up by class and the students raise the Cambodian flag and sing the national anthem. The song is sung halfheartedly, with little interest or pride. Tired and broken, the students reflect the hurting country outside these walls.

During my first class I have to enforce the "No-Khmer-speaking" rule;

no one is happy. I remind them that Cambodia Adventist School is an English-speaking school. They already seem to hate me. At least today I started them off early.

Gladly, I escape to my next class. The eleventh graders meet at the picnic tables across the small field because there aren't enough classrooms. Fortunately, there are only 11 students. This class likes me; they say I am pretty. I'll take what I can get.

The older the students are, the better their English is. That's why I especially enjoy the eleventh graders because they are the easiest to communicate with. The nine girls and two boys in this class are full of energy, smiles, and questions.

"Ms. Bo, do you have boyfriend? Ohhhhhhh!"

"Have you met Barack Obama?"

"Do think I can be in an American beauty pageant?"

In my next class the electrical power dies, so we have no lights, no fans. There are windows for natural light, but I definitely feel the absence of moving air. Thirty sweaty bodies in one confined space is a strong combination.

During a break, I walk to the restroom where I find a man fixing the doorknobs to the stalls. He quickly bows his head when he sees me, and he leaves to let me in. The stall I enter bears a circular hole where the doorknob used to be. I shut the door behind me. However, after I finish I try to open the door, but there is no door knob. Duh. I am locked in.

Standing on the toilet seat, waving my hand over the stall door with a string of pink toilet paper flitting in the breeze like an official restroom surrender, I yell, "Hello? Hello! Is anyone out there?" My voice echoes mournfully.

This continues for a few minutes before four maintenance workers appear. None of them speaks English, but they are speaking Khmer rapidly. I assume they are containing ridiculous laughter and saying to each other, "We had to rescue the American teacher from a toilet. I can't wait to tell everybody about this!"

I've made it through half my day. Now it's lunchtime. The cooks are Cambodian and, of course, do not speak English. Vegetarianism is a joke in Cambodia. Over half of their daily calories come from rice, but the rest is meat. The CAS kitchen is vegetarian, but it is full of unrecognizable vegetables and food that has been deep fried a few times.

The head cook, a small, wrinkly woman with a big grin, shoves something brown and fried toward me. I say, "Aw-tay," which means "no." The food is *supposed* to be vegetarian, but then again, the other day she handed me something brown and oily and with her hands made antlers above her head. I'm quickly learning to opt for food I recognize, when possible, vegetables and rice.

Later in my homeroom with the eighth graders a broken metal storage closet is moved out. Underneath, my students find a few baby mice. They swiftly sweep them up and jokingly push them toward my face. *Oh, that's funny.*

I try to settle my students down, and then the power goes out again. I'm thirsty and hot, but complaining is out of the question, especially when I think that some of these kids didn't get breakfast this morning.

By the end of the day I have raised my voice more than I wanted to. I made three seventh grade boys stay after class for talking during a quiz. I was not the teacher I wanted to be.

As the last student walks out the door, I lean against the podium in the empty classroom, drop my head, and begin to pray. A few students walk by, giggling. "Look, she is crying!"

I gather my things, dodge a lizard on my way out the door, and turn off the lights.

Teaching in Cambodia is just…different.

CHAPTER 8

Let's Be Honest, Shall We?

*"My grace is enough; it's all you need. My strength comes into its own in
your weakness. Once I heard that, I was glad to let it happen. I quit focusing
on the handicap and began appreciating the gift. It was a case of Christ's strength
moving in on my weakness. Now I take limitations in stride, and with good cheer,
these limitations that cut me down to size—abuse, accidents, opposition, bad
breaks. I just let Christ take over! And so the weaker I get, the stronger I become."*
—2 Corinthians 12:9, 10

Sitting alone tonight, I start thinking about the past 18 months and my
fight against an eating disorder—anorexia, to be exact.

Every week for the last year and a half, I have been seeing a counselor and
attending group sessions for other girls with eating disorders. When I say
"fighting" an eating disorder, I mean it. This has been an uphill battle ever
since it started my senior year of high school.

Growing up, I felt I held an identity I had to maintain. I was happy, pretty,
health nut Heather. Thus, I found myself unable to admit if I was ever having
a bad day; I was supposed to be happy. If I didn't look just right, I felt unable
to leave the house. I was supposed to be pretty. Occasionally, I would reach
for a slice of pizza, and someone would say, "Heather, you don't eat pizza!"
I was supposed to be a health nut.

My counselor has helped me realize that many people "should" themselves
to death:

"I shouldn't have dessert."

"I should exercise."

"I should make people happy."

"I should be a contented person."

I hate the word "should." Frankly, I don't use it anymore. I have missed
out on too many good things in life because of the shame I felt because

of who I should have been. After all, if I wasn't "happy, pretty, health nut Heather," who was I? I had no idea, and that terrified me.

There are no vacations in this fight. Not one day in 18 months. Anorexia is the hardest battle I have ever fought. Comparing it to my current situation in Cambodia is tricky. Is my experience in Cambodia harder than battling an eating disorder? I'm not sure. But battling an eating disorder in Cambodia, alone, sure tops the list right now.

Anorexia has been incredibly isolating. This is my battle, and I haven't cared to share it with others. Living in shame, I have kept it all inside. I imagine people finding out and saying, "What? Heather isn't the type to have an eating disorder! I thought she was a good person. I thought she had more faith in God than *that*."

If you were to walk into one of our ED (eating disorder) group sessions, you probably wouldn't know it. We all look normal. We come in different shapes and sizes. You can't always *see* health problems.

In group I met a girl named Jenny. She had been fighting her demon of anorexia since she was 10. Now, at age 30, she knew nothing else. And she looked the part. Jenny was bony and thin, fragile and pale. Her hair was falling out, her skin had turned sallow, and you could see her veins pulsing beneath transparent skin. No amount of makeup could cover her hollowness. She always looked exhausted, as if she hadn't slept in weeks. Really, she just hadn't eaten in days.

During the harsh Nebraska winters she had to use a blow-dryer in her apartment to keep herself warm because she didn't have enough fat on her body. That's how they found her.

Her parents walked into their daughter's apartment to find her facedown on the floor with the blow-dryer still running. Jenny never woke up. I visited her in the hospital. She existed in a coma for a week before she died.

After that weekend I realized that although I didn't *look* like Jenny, I *thought* like Jenny. That thought consumed my mind as I raced from one moment to the next, imagining how my life would end if I continued down this path. Something clicked. I realized I was sick and tired of pretending I was OK. I wasn't. I was sick and I was tired. It was time to admit it.

This revelation started me thinking about how many people live their lives in pain and isolation. I now believe that if everyone talked openly about their struggles, half their problems would vanish. Everyone has *something* they struggle with. I am much more honest and transparent with people now. I have nothing to lose and everything to gain. That is why I am writing these words.

Admitting I am human saved my life. I am not perfect. Right now, I am living in Cambodia, and I am struggling. On nights like tonight I want nothing more than a big hug from my parents. I want to cry to my sister, Ashley, and her husband, Ben. I wish I could wake up tomorrow at home, but here I sit.

Although I know I have a problem and I'm working through it, I still deal with my struggle every day. I wish I didn't have the urge to get up extra early to "run off" the calories I ate yesterday. Honestly, I wish I didn't have to eat tomorrow. I wish I didn't think this way. I wish I felt normal.

Silence is pain's best friend, but shame doesn't control my decisions anymore. I am realizing that the more I keep it inside, the more it hurts. I have lived long enough in isolation and pretense, and I am ready to move on, which is partly why I am in Cambodia. I have run away with God to reclaim and discover what I can be. The past is past.

Amazingly supportive family and friends have brought me here. Literally. Sometimes they sat and listened to me cry. Sometimes they took hold of my shoulders, shook me a bit, and brought me back to reality. I would not be sitting here if it weren't for them.

There is so much more to me than this battle, but I wouldn't give this recovery experience away for a billion dollars. If I don't help someone else or make a difference as a result of my struggle, then it has been completely wasted on me. I want this to matter. I want to know a purpose for hardships in my life. I wonder what that purpose is. *God, please help me know your plan.*

HIS-2

CHAPTER 9

Skin

"Culture is the widening of the mind and of the spirit."
—Jawaharlal Nehru

The Cambodian language is Khmer, and although 60 percent of Cambodians cannot read or write it, virtually all can speak it. And without fail, nasally, whiny sounds are apparently mandatory when speaking Khmer. Cambodians talk to one another with frowns and raise their shrill voices as if they are fighting. What are they saying? I have no idea, but their communication makes me cringe. They do not appear warm and cuddly. They might be very happy people, but they haven't notified their faces.

It is so hard adjusting to the culture in Cambodia. I'm learning something new every day. Asians are extremely loyal to their families, and they believe Americans aren't. I try explaining to them that what they see in the movies is usually far from the norm. But trying to convince them that I am actually close with and loyal to my family is basically impossible.

Marriage is an interesting union here. A Buddhist Khmer marrying a Christian Khmer will likely be disowned for ditching the family. However, a Khmer marrying a foreigner is good because they will have more money, but this engagement is allowed only if the couple promises to take care of their parents when they are old. Arranged marriages are more common than those made by choice. One of my tenth grade girls was at school one day and sent to be married the next. We haven't seen her since.

The natural progression of life is to have children after getting married, even if the family isn't able to care for them. Children pretty much run free here. Often when I am out at night, I see two or three little children playing in the light of a billboard, darting barefoot between cars. Once I saw a little girl, no more than 8 years old, sitting alone in the dark as the passing cars whizzed by. I wondered if her parents knew she was gone or if she had parents at all.

It's not difficult to see that I don't fit into their culture. Outside of the cultural differences, the color of my skin gives me away. Because foreigners get a lot of attention, whenever I sneeze, itch my ear, or yawn it is talked about and laughed at. This happens whether I am at school or on the street. I am constantly observed. So, I just pretend that I am at peace with feeling like a zoo animal and sneeze away.

The funny thing is that once Khmers get over the fact that I am white and in their presence, they are completely oblivious. When walking down the street, they won't move or acknowledge me until I am about to trip over them. If I am passing someone in a narrow area, they won't scoot over an inch.

Although white foreigners gain the most attention, black people are also of interest, just not in a good way. A lot of racism exists toward black people no matter where they're from. Cambodians with dark skin are either tormented or ignored. Dark Cambodians receive lower paying jobs or no job at all. Many people wear long-sleeve shirts, socks, and gloves to avoid showing their skin, not for health reasons, but for their pride.

At school one of the kindergartners is a little Indian girl. She is the only non-Khmer student at school, and she is ignored; none of the other kids even acknowledge her presence. It seems so unfair and unkind, so unlike how Christ would have acted.

I tell my students often that I think dark skin is beautiful and women back home actually pay money to lie in uncomfortable hot beds merely to make their skin darker. Many white people want to be tan, but Cambodians want to be white. It's ironic how our discontentment over beauty just depends on what part of the globe we are on.

CHAPTER 10

Disinterest, Disrespect, and Distance

"We take the good days from God—why not also the bad days?"
—Job 2:10

Mornings are hard. I suppose in the morning I have more time to think, so I do. I think about why in the world God has sent me here. I think about how much my back hurts from sleeping on a too-thin mattress. I think and dream about home, but I'm in Cambodia.

After I finish my morning musings, I head to school. My eighth graders are always waiting outside when I arrive. I can't get over the feeling that they are making fun of me in Khmer. Despite my discomfort, I smile and say "Good morning!" as I walk past.

My students have been fighting against the "No Khmer" rule during school. Instead of letting them do what they want at lunchtime, I recently had them stay at their desks until they spoke only English. The first day, they sat in complete silence because they refused to speak English. The next day, they "spoke" in grunts. They pointed and grunted and laughed hysterically—anything to avoid English. The next day, one-by-one they spoke enough English to ask to go to the bathroom after they ate; then they didn't return until lunchtime was over, 30 minutes later. Yesterday, three students set up their desks just outside the classroom in protest to the rule. They told me that since they weren't "in" the classroom, they shouldn't have to speak English. These kids are tricky.

I am 19 years old and not at all interested in playing their games. Was I this ridiculous in eighth grade? I'm tired of chasing them around. I'm tired of yelling. I don't know what to do with them. I know that their futures depend on learning English, but something has to change.

My second big struggle is my seventh graders. It is time for reading class, if you can call it that, but they don't want to be quiet. Actually, I'm not sure they have ever experienced quiet. Maybe there is no Khmer word for it. Either way, Ratana, a student in the front row, is a yeller. He doesn't speak; he yells, just to get attention. The other day I sang the James Brown oldie, "I feel good. I knew that I would. So good, so good, I've got you!" Ratana loved it. Unfortunately, I had no idea that randomly throughout class he would now be yelling, "SO GOOD! SO GOOD!"

In an effort to begin class, I divide the students into groups of three to read a story and answer questions on a worksheet. However, Ratana has a piece of cord he keeps whipping the students with in his group.

"Ow! Ms. Bo, Ratana hit me! Tell him stop!"

"Ratana, please stop whipping the girls. Give me that cord."

He backpedals, "No, I not do anything." He places the cord in his pocket, which is guaranteed to be used later. He swears that he forgot his book, again, so he can't read.   Another student, Hang Por, is a bit sneakier. Anytime I take my eyes off of him, he hits someone sitting next to him, crawls under his desk, and refuses to do whatever I ask of him. Hang Por draws pictures instead of reading and talks to anyone who will listen. He can't sit still. Amidst this chaos, some students are working quietly while others are falling asleep in the heat of the afternoon or cheating on their homework.

It's painful to watch kids like Ratana, Hang Por, and others as they struggle to sit in school. I am 98 percent positive that Ratana has ADHD. I feel helpless because I know it is more than stubbornness that keeps them from listening in class. Cambodia doesn't offer special programs for kids like this. So, eventually, they might get frustrated enough to quit and never come back. I also feel hopeless because I just don't have the time or skills to give the 100 kids I teach the direction they need.

I wish I could report that I am a fabulous teacher with excellent strategies and effective classroom management, but I'm not. I feel like I failed today. I lost my patience. I yelled. I got a headache. These kids don't like me, but I didn't come to Cambodia to make my students like me. I also didn't come to Cambodia to fight with my students for respect. So why did I come here?

Every day I ask God that question. But after another long day, I'm still waiting for an answer.

CHAPTER 11

Tired Teacher

"It is not our circumstances that create our discontent or contentment. It is us."
—Vivian Greene

Last night I tried to console myself with food, which ended up making me sick. I didn't sleep peacefully, and this morning I don't want to eat anything. As I talk to God, I plead for a good day, just one good day, to remind me that they exist and to give me strength for more rough days to come.

Today is busy. On eventful days like today I have less time to think about home. I have PE with the seventh graders I was so frustrated with yesterday. I realize that I was letting them decide whether I was going to have a good or a bad day. So today I take charge in PE, and I thoroughly wear them out instead.

"All right, everyone gather around. It's time to learn about cardiovascular fitness."

They stare at me, totally clueless as to what I just said. Sometimes I like to use big words they can't understand because it makes me feel better, you know, like maybe I am smart enough to teach them something.

"That means, instead of playing games or sitting around, we are going to run. Let's go!"

Strapping on a ridiculous grin, I lead them in our laps. Kids are crawling around the track by the time I am done with them. I'm serious. I didn't ask them to do anything I wasn't willing to do, so I know they weren't *actually* suffering. I run every lap they do. They are tired, and I am satisfied. Strangely enough, they are much calmer all day.

From here, I get another shot with the eighth graders. Lunchtime will be spent at their own desks because they spoke Khmer through study hall. But I say, "OK, let's play a game!"

They growl like two dozen caged lions, "No!" (At least the lions are speaking English!)

I tell them they can ask any questions of me that they want, as long as they speak English. They rise to the challenge.

"You have parents?"

"Do you have a boyfriend?"

"Have you met Britney Spears?"

"How old are you?"

I am surprised at their sudden interest. Maybe they have been waiting for this opportunity. Some of the boys start laughing so hard I think they forget they hate me. This time I am not chasing students around saying, "No Khmer!" It feels good to focus on having fun with the language. I can tell that they feel good.

I prayed. I received. It's easy to take this good day God has given me and assume that I did something to earn it. Maybe I have stumbled upon some magical method of teaching. Nah, I know better.

Thank you, God, for giving me this day. I needed it.

What I Thought I Wanted

*"So be content with who you are, and don't put on airs. God's strong
hand is on you; he'll promote you at the right time. Live carefree before
God; he is most careful with you."*
—1 Peter 5:6, 7

Most of the time I feel like this can't be real, this can't really be real. I assume I feel this way because I rarely feel like myself. Who is Heather? I'm adjusting to so many things, but I don't want to lose sight of what makes me me.

OK, so who am I? I am human first of all. I am a good listener and communicator. I like to smile. I am good at reading people. I am strong, independent, intelligent, curious, and somewhat adventurous. I can spend time with myself and still like myself. I like to read and journal. I like to explore. I have a good sense of direction. I like to try new things.

I like who I am, and I am willing to fight for it too. I stand up for myself and rarely do I leave things unsaid. I have never thought after a conversation, *Oh, I wish I would've said….* I am open and honest. I don't mind confrontation, so long as there is a good reason behind it, reasons like justice and peace. I like deepening relationships with history, not floating between groups and constantly making new acquaintances. I like community, consistency, and routine. I am athletic, playful, creative, and silly. I am capable; I can find my way and ask for what I need. I like to talk about things that matter. I like to learn and discuss. I like debates and real conversation. I like quotes. I like new ideas and thinking outside the box. I like who I am.

But it is so difficult to maintain a sense of self when no one within thousands of miles seems to know what that is or seems to know the real me.

I decided to be a student missionary in Cambodia because being with 20 other American college students seemed too easy. I decided to come alone.

I could have come with a friend, but I felt this was something I needed to do by myself. This was an adventure between God and me.

I came to Cambodia because I was weary of the American way of life: fast-paced, impersonal, media-saturated, selfish, scheduled, and nonstop. So here I am with lots of free time on weekends and vacations, and I'm still complaining. I see the Cambodian people just standing around all day. Honestly, some are up at 5:00 a.m. to do absolutely nothing all day long. But, instead of learning from or embracing their way of life, I get frustrated because my culture tells me I must always be doing something to matter.

I came to experience something new, a new way of life, but it is hard to shake old habits and behaviors. I knew there were going to be some adjustments, but I guess I just assumed the adjustments would be quicker or easier. This isn't immediate. It will take time. I have to be patient. I have to keep living.

CHAPTER 13

Changing Lives

"Be brave. Be strong. Don't give up. Expect God to get here soon."
—Psalm 31:24

I wake up with a sore throat and a sinus headache. First thought: What would Mom do? She put together a little first aid kit for me that included Airborne, vitamin C, and cold capsules. I remember her making me gargle with salt water whenever I had a sore throat. I cringe my way through the gargle as I always have, but it works.

At school I have promised my eighth graders that I will teach them the Macarena. This reminds me of a time at Union when Mr. Blake had us "dance" the Blakestep—more like marching in a circle—as we sang "King of Kings." Mr. Blake has never been afraid to be who he is and enjoy it in the process. I am enjoying myself too. They giggle through the Macarena, all the while thinking, This American is crazy!

Now to English class. I catch myself saying, "You are in the eleventh grade. You are almost seniors now. I expect more responsibility out of you." I hear it and nearly pinch myself.

I recall my eighth-grade teacher, Mrs. Shockley, saying, "Come on. You are the oldest students at this school. You need to act like it."

I finish my speech. I am half-angry, half-laughing.

From here I go to my newest class, first-grade reading. Thirty-two little first graders wiggle around in their seats. Very few can actually read, but all of them can repeat what the smartest kid in class says, so they do. I work with them one-on-one to assess where they are in their reading skills. Today, we are learning words like *mat, sat, let, bet*—all the good old short vowel sounds. As they practice writing these words, I keep walking by and noticing Udom, a pudgy, quiet boy in the back, struggling. As the class ends, I check on him, and he is still quite far from finishing.

I kneel next to his desk and place my hand on his back, "How are you doing? See all of these big letter As? They need to be little letter As."

He looks at me exhaustedly and reaches for his eraser for the twenty-eighth time this class period.

"Here," I say, "let's do it together."

As we struggle through writing lowercase letter As, he eventually completes it. I clap my hands. I smile and praise him, "Good job, Udom! You are such a smart boy! I am so proud of you."

I hope he is proud of himself. I hope I am doing for him what my sister, Ashley, and her husband, Ben, do for me. Every small accomplishment deserves praise. They have lifted me up by their encouraging words more times than I can count. They have shown me the power of affirming human touch.

The day is rolling right along, and now I'm off to my tenth-grade English class. Today, their final personal narratives—a one-page typed paper—are due; this is a big deal. They have really struggled with the assignment, even though they could pick their own topic. As the deadline arrives, I am still missing six papers. A motley collection of excuses rain on me: computer glitches, empty printer cartridges, forgotten at home, lost on a jump drive. Two girls look as though they are about to cry.

"Do any of you know the meaning of the word 'grace'?"

They shake their heads no, wondering what nonsense I'm talking about now.

"Grace is something that we don't necessarily deserve, but we receive it anyway. Have you heard of the grace of God? Amazing grace? I am giving you grace. If your papers are in my hand tomorrow, you won't lose any points."

I make each of them pinky-promise me that I will have the paper tomorrow. I continue, "Now, by grace we are changed. If your papers are late the next time and the next time, then you are abusing the gift of grace. I will be more hesitant to give it to you if it doesn't change your behavior in some way."

As soon as I started the "grace" speech, I knew where it was headed. I didn't even have to think about it. I myself had been "gracified" before. My high school chemistry teacher, Mr. Harold Williams, "gracified" me on more than one occasion when I forgot an assignment. I was changed. Obviously.

Another class down, and more to go. Eighth grade geography is next. In all honesty I am not prepared for this class. The material I am supposed to cover, I hardly understand myself. How in the world do equinoxes and the 365-and-one-fourth-day revolution of the earth around the sun affect me, anyway? Dumb question, I know. But it is so confusing and always has been.

Since I suspect that some of my students may know more about this than I do, I just start asking a lot of questions. This is way more fun.

"Aliyah, will you please help me with an example?" I ask.

He stands up confidently.

"I need another helper. Let's see." I spot Vanny throwing paper out the window. "Vanny, why don't you come help me?"

I face them in front of the class and put my arms around their shoulders. "You see, Aliyah is the sunshine. Isn't he shiny?"

He plasters a giant smile on his face and lifts his arms to the sides. Laughter erupts at his acting.

"And Vanny is the earth."

A clever student in the back pipes up: "Ms. Bo, we live on earth. So I go jump on Vanny?" More giggles.

"Um, we're just pretending. *Imagine* you are living on Vanny, OK?"

Simulating the sun and the earth's rotations, Vanny walks circles around Aliyah, and Aliyah occasionally tips Vanny off his axis by nudging him out of orbit. The rest of the class is cracking up so hard buttons may start popping off their shirts. They get the picture.

Mr. Nobuhara, my high school biology teacher, made learning fun, so it never felt like learning. I can only hope for Mr. Nob's results.

Today I was keenly aware of just how much of who I am is a direct result of someone else. I am blessed. I have an incredible network of friends and family who have taught me, prayed with me, and lived with me. The distance does not separate us as much as it feels sometimes. I owe so much of who I am to those who have influenced my life.

Often I am reminded of loved ones at some point in my day: a song on my iPod we sang together, a lesson in school I didn't get then and I still don't get now, or maybe just a comment someone said to me.

I didn't get to this point in my life by myself. Thanks for leading me here.

CHAPTER 14

Where ADRA Works

"Knowledge is knowing that we cannot know."
—*Ralph Waldo Emerson*

I wake up this morning and stubbornly think, I don't want to be in Cambodia today. I must have had another dream about home.

Fortunately, it is Sunday, and I can "call" my family and friends. I am at the Internet shop at 9:00 a.m., trying to figure out Skype so that I can talk with Ashley and Ben. It works, and I am able to connect to them, my parents in Colorado, and a friend in Washington. I can't complain. With technology at my fingertips, compared to student missionaries 20 years ago, I am still connected to home.

My family knows my history, my strengths, my weaknesses; they know me. Because they care, they genuinely ask me, "How are you doing?"

After our talks, I feel really good. But alas, Sundays are grading days. I always have schoolwork to do, lesson plans to write, and papers to grade. So I bury myself in work.

I know now that I sought to be an SM because I wanted to say, "I was a student missionary in Cambodia for a year." I am not sure it is worth it to make that claim. There is a huge difference between *wanting* to be an SM and actually *doing it*. There is a huge difference between being inspired by an ADRA video and being inspired enough to serve the people on it. There is a huge difference between saying I love people and actually loving them.

Ly Chard is a first grader at CAS. He actually lives across the street from me. All in all, he is a good kid with decent English and a big toothy grin. He is a little shrimp who prefers to go shirtless most of the time and likes attention. When his sweaty little self wants to play airplane and jump off tables into my arms, I don't always want to play.

He has a paper crown that says, "Today is my birthday." He wears it every day. On the inside is written: "Ly Chard, Happy Birthday. Here in America children like these sorts of things. Hope you enjoy it too!"

Ly Chard is a sponsored child. You know, the children you can sign up for in foreign countries and write letters to? That is Ly Chard. I don't know how many of my students have American sponsors. Several, I am sure. This reminds me of the difference between writing a child letters and sending gifts, and actually being here loving them and catching their sweaty little bodies.

Where I live is not a beautiful place. There's nothing glamorous about teaching in a hot classroom surrounded by 30 sweaty bodies. There's nothing particularly "cool" about walking past beggars without legs and children without clothes. The language barrier is awful and isolating. Being labeled "foreigner" gets old, fast. Yet I am and always will be.

I don't say this to be demeaning. I don't want to discourage people from sponsoring children in other countries or sending money to ADRA. However, I have come to realize that the things I thought would be rewarding because I was doing them for God are not guaranteed to be easy. It isn't always an adventure. There is a difference between talking and doing.

Henry Ford said, "You cannot build a reputation on what you are going to do."

Preach it, Henry.

CHAPTER 15

Breakdown

*"He heals the heartbroken and bandages their wounds. He counts
the stars and assigns each a name. Our Lord is great, with limitless strength;
we'll never comprehend what he knows and does. God puts the fallen on their
feet again and pushes the wicked into the ditch."*
—Psalm 147:3-6

As an alcoholic reaches for alcohol to numb the pain, I reach for food. Anorexia has turned into bulimia, a common transition according to my counselor. So where I used to starve myself to feel in control of life's craziness, now I eat to numb the pain and loneliness. But that "high" lasts only so long, until I am sick and wanting to throw up.

I don't know how to stop this awful cycle.

After a night feeling horribly alone, fat, ugly, pathetic, disgusting, incapable, inadequate and everything between, I cry myself to sleep. I wake up weak and exhausted. I pray a desperate prayer for strength and head downstairs to my bike.

Today the tears won't stop. I climb on my bike and start to cry. Crying lately seems as natural as breathing.

I ride past the guard and cry. I pass the waiting moto drivers and cry. I cycle past the locals just starting their day and cry. I don't carry a few moist tears in my eyes; I am all-out, holding-nothing-back sobbing. The Cambodians always stare at me; at least today they have a good reason.

I make it to school and try to gather myself. As I walk toward my classroom, the thought of standing in front of my students terrifies me, and I start crying again. Four students wait outside the classroom. They become awkwardly quiet. I walk in, shut the door behind me, and weep so bitterly it actually hurts. My chest aches from the pressure, and my entire body tenses with every gasp.

I'm sure my students can hear me through the thin walls, but I can't stop.

I nearly fall over as I reach my desk. I catch myself with both hands and bend over at the waist, pasting my forehead to my desk. Hyperventilation takes over, and I can't catch my breath. Gasping for air, I sit down and force myself to breathe. It is time for staff worship.

Quickly passing my students on the way out the door, I find a seat in the back at worship, but I don't last long. The only place I can think of going is to the bathroom, which is where girls seem to go in times of distress. I find an empty stall, sit down, and cry. A few minutes later, Fay finds me. She holds me for several moments before I can actually form sentences.

"I can't do this anymore," I choke out. "It's too painful. This is not what I thought it would be. I come to school every day; I do my best, but it's never good enough. I don't understand this culture. I spend all day surrounded by people, and yet, I still feel alone. No one understands me or cares that I'm here. I get through an exhausting day, am stared at the whole way home, then sit alone in the apartment, and wish I were around people who love me. I feel invisible and unimportant. I'm just not strong enough for this." The sobs return.

It feels good to talk, but I am still alone. Fay holds me and says she is sorry. What else can she do?

Like it or not, I have to go on with the day. Teachers and students uncomfortably glance in my direction not knowing what to do or say.

I didn't intentionally cry my eyes out this morning, and I can't break down every time I need something, but my feelings were so overwhelming. I couldn't hold them in anymore. I tried to stuff it inside, suck it up, and go on. But it didn't work today; I let my emotions take over.

I am still struggling with trying to be perfect instead of letting my guard down and being real. Hopefully after today's breakdown I'm headed in the right direction. I am not OK, and I can't expect help unless I ask for it.

I am doing what I can with what I have. I need to remember that I cannot blame anyone for my life. I have to be an active agent, not a spectator. I can't let circumstances, people, or places decide my life for me. I am trying desperately to live with purpose. Maybe I am on my way.

God, please keep helping me. I have so much to learn.

CHAPTER 16

Falling Off the Rug

"Wait, Israel, for God. Wait with hope. Hope now; hope always!"
—*Psalm 131:3*

Schools in Cambodia let out this week for the annual Pechum Ben holiday, a Buddhist celebration. During Pechum Ben people wake up at 4:00 a.m. every morning, walk to a pagoda, and throw rice at it in order to feed their dead ancestors who are hungry. They believe that spirits come out once a year to eat, and if they are not fed they will curse the entire family.

At staff worship yesterday the principal strongly recommended staying close to home. Pechum Ben is a week honoring the dead. The spirits are invited into the city and worshipped.

It's Monday, the first day of the celebration, and I decide to venture out despite the principal's warning. I take an eerie walk in the rain. Most of the shops are closed and only a few people are wandering outside, a noticeable and unsettling difference from the usual chaos of the streets.

Later that day a CAS teacher named JC informs me, "Last month I met a witch. She knew I was Christian and told me that her spirits were greater than God. The spirits give her wealth, she said, and immediately she started grabbing at her throat and coughing violently. After a few minutes she appeared to vomit a red gemstone, which she placed in my hand."

These types of stories and experiences remind me of how real the battle is between good and evil.

Although the spirit world is a big part of Cambodian culture—some of my students wear red spirit strings around their wrists, ankles, and waists to ward off evil spirits—many people don't seem to care about what Buddhists believe. From what I can gather, being Buddhist here is like being an American. You don't have to know the fourteenth president, the Constitution, and the Pledge of Allegiance backwards to be an American; you are an American because of where you were born and live. Out of nearly 400 students at Cambodia Adventist School, only 10 percent are Adventists. When I ask students what Buddhists believe, none of them really knows.

In much the same way, my students ask me, "Ms. Bo, what is it like in New York City?"

"Umm, I'll let you know when I see it."

Astonished, they ask, "You never go to New York City? But you are America!"

"Well, actually I am *American*, but that doesn't mean I've seen everything in *America*."

Students generally just see this holiday as a break from school. Unfortunately, for me downtime, holidays, and weekends are hard, so I try to stay busy.

On Wednesday I do a little reading and some much needed laundry before heading to the Russian market. This city block of shops and vendors is constantly crawling with people yelling and selling. Cambodia supplies the U.S. with products from brands such as Northface, Gap, Hollister, and American Eagle. So, for cheap clothes and pirated DVDs, look no further than the Russian market. They also sell tourist trinkets and toys.

The area around the Russian market is heavily populated by NGOs, or nongovernmental organizations. Other than the Russian market area, we are the signature foreigners and feel it every day.

On Thursday Fay invites me to come over and cook. Apparently she doesn't mind cleaning but hates cooking. I am thrilled to help. We drive to the market to pick up a few ingredients so that I can make chocolate chip cookies, bread, and carrot cake. It's so nice to have a stocked kitchen and familiar food at Fay's house; it makes it feel a little more like home.

Unfortunately, although I was looking forward to cooking earlier, right now I'm feeling panicky and irrational. This is turning in to one of those days where I hate being around food—I hate smelling it, talking about it, and especially eating it. In the same way you wouldn't leave an alcoholic alone in a bar, I fear being left alone in the kitchen. My mind starts racing; food becomes the enemy.

Fay is content cleaning the refrigerator. She has no idea the inner struggle I'm experiencing right now. Fortunately, her presence gives me some sense of security, and I try to fight past the battle in my mind.

It turns out a change of scenery didn't make everything better. I'm realizing that I can't run away from this eating disorder. It goes where I go. Sometimes I feel toxic to myself, which is a miserable feeling. I can't seem to run away from my thoughts and struggles.

On Friday I enter a wireless restaurant with intentions of doing some schoolwork. But when I see my sister, Ashley, online, I start chatting with her.

At the start of our conversation, I am in pretty good spirits. I figure we would talk for a few minutes, but we chat for quite a while, and an hour later I am crying as the waiters watched me uncomfortably. Why the sudden change?

During the course of our conversation, I brought up the option the principal gave me of coming home a month early to attend graduation or get back for a summer job. I don't know anyone in particular graduating, and I don't have a job to race back to.

So Ashley asked, "Do you need to come home early for something in particular, or are you just looking for an excuse?"

I knew the answer.

She continued, "You don't have to stay in Cambodia if you don't want to. But will you regret it if you don't?"

Part of me doesn't want to ever fit in here. I rarely think about staying the entire ten months. I'm just waiting to see how long I'll last.

I have been here about eight weeks, but I continue to try to live in two places at once. I sleep in Cambodia, but I dream about home. I work in Cambodia, but I work even harder staying in touch with friends back home. I talk to God in Cambodia, but usually I am praying that everyone back home won't forget about me. I laugh in Cambodia, but often it's about something funnier that happened back home.

I imagine the countries as two rugs. I am most comfortable with the rug I have lived on my whole life—the U.S. As soon as I boarded the plane to come to Cambodia, the U.S. rug was ripped from underneath me. Then, 20 hours later, I was plopped on this threadbare, smelly piece of carpet where I live now. I find myself trying to keep one foot on the home rug and one foot on this new rug. But I can't have both. I know I can't have both because when I think I can, both rugs are pulled away and I land on my butt, hard. Then I feel homeless—as I do right now.

I can't live this way all year. It isn't possible. I will never be totally here if I insist on trying to straddle both worlds. The spiritual parallels are obvious, aren't they? Trying to serve two masters, living in two kingdoms. And, as a result, feeling homeless.

I have yet to fully embrace this country, my work, the other teachers, the church, the locals, the environment—everything that is Cambodia.

CHAPTER 17

Youran

"He always does what he says—he defends the wronged, he feeds the hungry.
God frees prisoners—he gives sight to the blind, he lifts up the fallen."
—Psalm 146:6-8

Today is the first day back at school after vacation. I arrive armed with a few new rules. From now on, everyone will definitely call me Ms. Bo. Most of them do anyway, but the problem comes when every teacher is simply called "Teacher," so every time a student calls out in a crowd about 20 teachers turn their heads.

Also, I figured out that of the 36 hours each week my eighth graders spend at school only six hours are spent with me. As much as they complain about my "No Khmer" rule during my classes, they are being asked to speak English only 16.6 percent of the entire week of classes. I tell them that if they can go five days in a row doing their best to speak only English, I will reward them. I wasn't specific about the reward because I have no idea what it will be. Today they do really well.

I hear them helping each other. "Hey, please don't speak Khmer! Remember what Ms. Bo said? We can get a prize!"

I'm worried. I may have to actually find a reward for them by the end of the week. We'll see.

And the last new rule: no complaining. I am tired of it. If I hear one complaint during class, the assignment will immediately get doubled, no questions asked. I already implemented the rule today when the tenth graders were picking roles for the Christmas play. Phalkun, the first girl who complained, is playing Mary. Congratulations!

In English class my tenth graders are doing presentations on books they have read. They had the option to draw a picture and tell about it, write a song, or give an oral presentation. I purposely added the drawing option for a student named Youran. He is an incredible artist but painfully shy. I am excited to see his art as I ask him to go next.

He shuffles in his flip-flops to the front of the room, looks directly at the floor in front of him, and mumbles.

"Youran, can you please speak a little louder? Thank you."

He continues muttering and holds his drawings behind his back. As soon as he brings his hands forward, the students start heckling.

His hands shake so uncontrollably we can't even see the outline of his drawings. He seems equally surprised and embarrassed; his bottom lip quivers. I think he is going to cry. Still, he manages an uncomfortable smile and continues mumbling as the students try to contain their chuckling.

A student in the back pipes up, "Ms. Bo, can *I* hold Youran's drawings so he'll stop shaking?"

The entire class erupts in laughter. Youran lowers his head, humiliated, and stares at the ground.

I stop everything and stand next to Youran.

"Do any of you enjoy getting up in front and giving presentations?"

They all shake their heads, no.

"Standing in front of people takes a lot of courage, and you are all making it horribly difficult for Youran. Please, please let him finish and stop being so rude."

They drop their heads and apologize, though still smirking.

I whisper to Youran, "OK, let's take some deep breaths. In... and out... ahhhh. You want to try again?"

His hands continue to shake, but he makes it through. When he is done, I jump out of my chair, clap loudly, hoot and holler, and thank him repeatedly.

"Youran, I hereby give you permission to laugh and scoff and humiliate any of these tenth graders at any point during their presentations, OK?"

I know he won't, but I wink at him, and he gives me a smile of relief.

Youran won't always be so painfully shy; I'm sure of it.

After school as I am grading papers, a large rat scurries above me on the rafters. I secretly hope it will fall and be chopped up into a hundred pieces by the ceiling fan below. Then I realize that would be gross, and I would just have to clean it up anyway.

Some days are more interesting than others. Regardless, today, for the first time, I actually consider staying here the entire 10 months. Imagine that.

CHAPTER 18

The Big Three

*"There is no medicine like hope, no incentive so great, and no tonic
so powerful as expectation of something better tomorrow."*
—*Orison S. Marden*

I must be disintegrating. My hair has been falling out since I got here. Weakness overwhelms my legs, and I have to really fight to make it up the stairs to my apartment at the end of each day. No amount of sleep ever seems to be enough. True rest is a joke. My health is less than stellar.

I read Genesis 22 this morning where God tells Abraham to sacrifice Isaac. As Abraham is about to kill his son, an angel appears and says these words, "Now I know how fearlessly you fear God; you didn't hesitate to place your son, your dear son, on the altar for me." As a result of Abraham's faithfulness to God, the angel of the Lord continues, "I swear—God's sure word!—because you have gone through with this, and have not refused to give me your son, your dear, dear son, I'll bless you—oh, how I'll bless you!"

I thought, Wow, I would love to hear those words from God at the end of this experience. That would make it all worth it. To hear God say, "Heather, because you have gone through this painful experience and have not refused to dedicate yourself to me—oh, how I'll bless you!"

So what am I willing to place on the altar for God? What will I have to endure this year? It scares and exhausts me to think that there is no guarantee that the hardest part is behind me. I have no idea what lies ahead of me.

I have been talking about the prayer of Jabez with my eighth graders in worship each morning. Some mornings I read and dare them to ask big things of God like Jabez did. I tell them that they will only get big results if they ask big things of God.

Vitya says, "Ms. Bo, I am start ask God for helicopter!"

The class clown comes through again, and the whole class is now as hysterical as a circus.

"Well, Vitya. That is not exactly how it works. I am not saying that God *cannot* give you a helicopter, but sometimes He *will not*. God has a plan and while He loves us, He knows what we *want* and what we really *need*."

The whole class was still stuck on the helicopter idea, though. This was not the first time I wondered if they really heard me.

Pondering my life, I don't think I am asking enough of God. I pray with desperation, "God, just get me through this meal. I don't want to eat today." But maybe I'm missing something. So I start thinking more specifically about what would be an extravagant request of God. Not helicopter requests, but big none the less. What would at first seem silly or ridiculous to ask God for? I quickly think of three requests—I decide to call them the "big three" and pray them daily. If God is willing to hear me, I'm willing to keep asking, even as humongous as they seem.

My first extravagant request is that I want to leave my eating disorder in Cambodia. I can't continue my life this way. Too often I imagine fighting this forever, spending lonely night after lonely night crying myself to sleep.

"I can't do this alone, Father. I've tried. I'm not getting anywhere. Please take this away from me. I have hopes for a better life, but I can't have it without You."

My second request is that I want people to care that I am here. I need to feel support from someone, anyone. I need a friend.

"I can't get through this year feeling like no one cares that I am here. Please, send someone. Send anyone who will care."

My last request is that I want to know that there is a purpose for why I am here. I want to matter. I want to know that I am doing something important.

"God, I need to know that this is all worth it. I need to know a reason you have brought me here."

I am being bold with God. What if He has been waiting for me to ask for these things? I will pray and do my balanced best to make the changes I can along the way, but the rest is in His hands. I cannot do this alone.

"Please come through for me, God. Please."

It's Thursday, my busiest school day. The other days I have one or two class periods off, but Thursdays are nonstop. I head to class in the cool morning weather. It's probably 70 degrees, but my kids pile on the clothing layers and talk about the "goods bumps" on their skin. I'd like some goods bumps!

My third class period is first-grade reading. The seventh graders and first graders are probably tied right now for "Most Difficult Class to Teach." It is hard enough teaching first grade in the U.S., but only two of my 23 students speak semiunderstandable English. They all know basic utilitarian words like: teacher, bathroom, finished, and their own names. They are also perfect little parrots. They can repeat anything I say to them. But do they understand? Oh, that would be too easy.

Today I write on the board: On your paper write the word "man" three times. As I collect their papers, many of them have written all over it "man three times."

As I walk around the classroom, each student says, "Teacher Header," and gazes at me as I walk by their desk. They don't have a question. They don't need anything. They just want to be noticed. They say, "Teacher Header," grin, and usually point to a picture they are coloring.

"Oh, how pretty! Keep coloring!" I reply to every student as I walk by.

One first grade student named Lassa is the tiniest boy. He hardly fills his small plastic chair. His head barely peeks over his desk. All Cambodians have dark black hair. Lassa's hair is light brown. Light hair is a sign of malnourishment, the best indicator to tell which students are the poorest—that and how irregularly their school bill gets paid.

I watch Lassa from across the room as other children play happily around him. He sits quietly, unlikely to move or join in with their games. Sadness has already moved into his young body, and he hardly musters a smile. It is hard to help him focus, and I feel bad asking him to.

Most mornings the students don't get breakfast, which explains why they are irritable and ravenous. If I see students without a lunch, I know that I am in for an even tougher afternoon. Of course they are difficult to teach. Some of them may be starving.

It's overwhelming to know that I can't possibly help all of them. It's heartbreaking to realize some of my students haven't eaten all day. It's exhausting watching my students with learning disabilities struggle through class every day. It's hard to see them sit in class feeling hopeless.

While I am asking God for big things in my life, my students are slipping through the cracks and there seems to be little I can do.

CHAPTER 19

Sugar Cane Juice

"Those who think they can do it on their own end up obsessed with measuring their own moral muscle but never get around to exercising it in real life. Those who trust God's action in them find that God's Spirit is in them—living and breathing God! Obsession with self in these matters is a dead end; attention to God leads us out into the open, into a spacious, free life."
—Romans 8:5, 6

God, send me someone, anyone who cares enough to ask, 'How are you?' because I am not OK. I'm tired, beat up, and falling apart. Are You listening?"

Today, I am asking my second big thing of God, and I need an answer.

As I walk into the compound after a long day at school, Sylvia, who lives and works here at the mission, stops me and says, "Heather, how are you?"

I stutter, amazed that someone has actually asked. "Umm, I'm . . . uh . . . I'm not the best. Actually, I'm having a *really* hard time."

Sylvia and her husband, Garth, are British and have the most adorable accents. She asks and then, amazingly, she really listens. We swap stories, and I share some of my struggles with her. She invites me over at 5:30 p.m. for "tea," which apparently means dinner.

No way am I going to miss this. I arrive and instantly feel at home. Their place is nicely furnished, air-conditioned, and peaceful. They have a Sabbath ritual that I am glad to follow: Sabbath candles, prayer, supper, talking, singing, reading Bible passages—this is exactly what I need.

It is so calming to just "be" with them. Real conversation is like bandages for my wounds. I don't end up talking much. I just want to listen to them tell their unbelievable mission stories. They have been in Iceland, Pakistan, Sri Lanka, Cambodia, and the list goes on. The peaceful atmosphere envelops me. There's not much peace in my one-room apartment shared with two other girls. There just isn't. This feels more like home. I sincerely hope they'll invite me over again sometime.

It is Sabbath morning, and I am up at 6:30 a.m., so I head outside for a walk. As I come back, my roommates are heading out the door.

"Hey, we're going to do evangelism at a church in the provinces."

Instantly, as they leave I realize that same calm I felt the night before. I am alone and it is beautiful. I am rarely alone in our apartment. I had every intention of going to Sabbath school, but everything about that peaceful apartment tells me to stay put. I shower, enjoy the quiet, praise God for His answer to my prayer, journal, and read. *Ahhhh!*

After a while I go downstairs to the Khmer church service just below me. Finding some familiar faces, I sit down with them. My eleventh graders are leading song service. I feel so proud when I see my students doing something up front. They could simply be sitting on stage and I'd want to applaud wildly.

The service is surprisingly interesting and applicable. First of all, it is translated into English, which is rare. Also, the talk is being given by an energetic CAS teacher I really like.

I sit with another CAS teacher named JC. He is 27, friendly, kind, and an all-around good guy. After church I meet JC downstairs. We are going to ride his moto to another province about an hour away and visit a zoo.

We load up and put on helmets, sunglasses, and breathing mask. It feels so good to leave the congestion of the city. I never see greenery anywhere. You may think I am overexaggerating, but come visit. I am serious. Phnom Penh is made up of concrete, dirt roads, and chaos. Getting out to the country is a long ride, over an hour. Hot and sweaty, my helmet hangs heavy on my head. My butt is sore and my mouth dry. Yet, a smile sets up camp on my face and won't go away. I am leaving the city. I don't have to think. I don't have to entertain, please, teach, mediate, or communicate. Right now, I just have to sit and ride.

Rice paddies dot the fields of tall grass. Scattering the horizon, palm trees resemble giants. I imagine them as the rulers in this countryside where government doesn't seem to reach.

"These are the Kampoung people," JC yells over his shoulder. "They have lived in the country their whole lives. They've never been to school or seen the city. They are simple and don't know any English."

Living in wooden shacks on stilts, they farm the land for all their food. Hearing JC describe an even simpler version of the Cambodians from the city makes me chuckle.

"Americans aren't good at relaxing, myself included," I admit. "We have schedules and like things a certain way. It's sad because I wonder if Cambodians are happier the way they live. Americans seem to think they have it all together."

I know I am becoming much more laid back the longer I am here. Being on time is not important here—everyone is late. Friends pay for each other and don't ask to be paid back. People say "Stop by anytime" and mean it because they are almost always at home.

The zoo is more of an animal reserve. Unlike American zoos, there are no sidewalks, labeled exhibits, or clean cages. Here you can reach into the cages and the monkeys can grab your hair, which happens to JC. I just laugh because he is crazy for getting that close anyway.

The sad part is that the cages are small and onlookers throw their trash at the animals. Little children taunt the animals who are limping or missing limbs. Some cages don't have signs, so we have no idea what is inside. Still, JC is thrilled, and I am happy just to be out of the city.

On the way back, we stop at a roadside stand, and I taste some jackfruit. This is my new favorite food. Jackfruit is huge, larger than a watermelon, and it hangs from a tree. Inside are bright yellow sections that taste like a banana and a mango. I will definitely want more during my time here.

I pass on the fried frog legs and hanging animals, which are dripping blood and attracting flies. My butt is really sore, so I make a few excuses to stop and take pictures. I capture a few malnourished cows and naked children on my camera. On we go through the countryside, then into the city again.

This time we ride along the riverside, which is always busy with street vendors and people playing games. Our last stop is insisted upon by JC.

"You've got to try sugar cane juice. They take the sugar cane rods and crank them through these metal rollers to press all the juice out."

The sugar cane juice is deliciously sweet, cool, and refreshing after a long day in the sun.

It still feels like this can't be real. It must be a dream, but for the first time, I mean that in a good way. Today, I think again about staying. I may never fit in or look the part of a native Cambodian; I will always be white. However, my head and my heart are filling with incredible experiences I will never forget. I am learning my way around the city, and I now know the Khmer words I need to use when traveling. It is funny to see the foreigners who are obviously weekend tourists and know I am not one of them.

I am not visiting. I am here to stay awhile. I work here. This is my reality. I am not coming and going.

I am finding my place.

CHAPTER 20

Ninety-two Things

"Anyone who intends to come with me has to let me lead. You're not in the driver's seat—I am. Don't run from suffering; embrace it. Follow me and I'll show you how. Self-help is no help at all. Self-sacrifice is the way, my way, to finding yourself, your true self."
—*Luke 9:23, 24*

The Cambodian countryside passes by as we travel to a southern beach town called Sihanoukville. I see shelters on stilts above ponds of sewage, white emaciated cattle, small children casting fishing nets, and towering palm trees along the rice fields. My roommates and I boarded the bus this morning to escape Phnom Penh for a short vacation from school.

A Khmer movie with Chinese subtitles plays loudly on the bus as I watch soldiers shoot and yell at each other on the screen. It looks like the Cambodian version of *M*A*S*H*. A woman behind me answers her cell phone and shouts in a language I don't recognize. The bus driver spends most of his time honking at motos and trucks packed with garment workers headed to the factories.

I sit next to a man from Spain who seems comfortable as a traveler. He has seen so much of the world, a broad perspective. I can't always understand everything he is saying in his broken English, so I focus on his lips and nod my head and smile.

He says, "I've seen breathtaking landscapes on the coast of Greece and beautiful countrysides in Florence, Italy, that are indescribable."

"That sounds gorgeous!" I say. "It can be so hard to find beauty in Cambodia, especially in the city!"

"Oh, the beauty is here. You just have to look for it. The character and values, culture and smiles of this country are infectious."

Is this man crazy? Honestly I think it all sounds a bit clichéd because I was hoping he would tell me about some hidden part of Cambodia I hadn't found yet. But he didn't.

The beauty here *is* harder to see. In America ideal conditions, beautiful landscapes, and easy living have been handed to me. Is my situation here completely devoid of beauty, or am I missing something? Am I missing out on a great adventure because part of me refuses to adjust?

I will not live in Cambodia for the rest of my life. I am not trapped. I am not suffering. I did not sign up for easy, ideal, or beautiful. I signed up for Cambodia and everything that entails. I may never find this place to be charming, but I need to accept my reality and start living.

Faults are always easy to spot, but what about the good things? What do I *like* about my life here? I decide to make a list:

- wearing less makeup, spending less time on my hair, my wardrobe
- doing all of my own grocery shopping
- riding motos to get around town
- Asian pears
- fresh sugarcane juice
- being called "Ms. Bo"
- a simpler life
- the funny sounds Cambodians make when they laugh really hard
- the kindergarten girls when they come out of the bathroom with their uniforms tucked into their underwear
- the beautiful Buddhist temples
- watching my students perform, get up front, sing, anything
- traveling, eating, and buying clothes cheaply
- my 6-year-old Pakistani neighbor who calls me "Baji Heather," which means "sister"
- wearing Crocs every day
- seeing monks riding motos
- living where ADRA works
- the smiley cook in the kitchen at CAS (we don't speak the same language, but we still communicate)
- Cambodian dancing
- dragon fruit
- meeting people from all over the world

• the random herd of goats that wanders around my neighborhood I continue writing as we ride along. By the time I'm done with my list, I've written down 92 things that I like about my life in Cambodia.

Arriving in Sihanoukville, we find a guesthouse on the ocean, drop our things, and go swimming. The beach isn't crowded, but in Cambodia all the locals wear jeans and long-sleeved shirts to swim. This makes my one-piece swimsuit look a bit risqué.

The next day we relax at the beach in the morning, visit some waterfalls, and even splurge on foot massages, which cost only four dollars.

After two days in Sihanoukville, we head back to Phnom Penh. It was an incredibly relaxing and much needed getaway.

Make Sihanoukville number 93 on the list.

HIS-3

CHAPTER 21

Double Takes

"So here's what I want you to do, God helping you: Take your
everyday, ordinary life—your sleeping, eating, going-to-work, and
walking-around life—and place it before God as an offering. Embracing
what God does for you is the best thing you can do for him. Don't become
so well-adjusted to your culture that you fit into it without even thinking.
Instead, fix your attention on God. You'll be changed from the inside out.
Readily recognize what he wants from you, and quickly respond to it."
—*Romans 12:1, 2*

The longer I live here, the more things become "normal" to me. At first the cultural differences shocked me, but the more I'm surrounded by them, the more they seem like the norm.

Public flirting is practically breaking the law. It is a disgrace to the family. However, it is quite acceptable for boys to hold hands with boys. Is that what they hoped to achieve with that unwritten law?

Although it no longer surprises me the lack of space between people and vehicles, I must need more space than others. A moto actually grazed my hip as I was jogging the other day. It makes me want to randomly swing my arms in circles so maybe someday I will "accidentally" clothesline someone on a passing moto driving way too close. Is that mean? I guess I have a bubble and they don't.

Everyone here rides motos, which are not motorcycles but are more like mopeds. You can pay a driver to take you anywhere you want. Since I am a woman, I am expected to ride sidesaddle. It's a culture thing. Today, on the back of a moto, I juggle two bags of groceries while sitting sidesaddle and wearing a backpack and an oversized helmet. I must have incredibly good balance, because there is nothing to hold on to back here. I guess I am adapting.

Fortunately, my moto driver can keep both of his hands on the handlebars. That isn't always the case. Very often you will see a moto driver holding an IV bag for the passenger sitting behind him. People here are convinced that an IV can cure anything from the common cold to a headache. So if they can afford to see a doctor, they get an IV.

In spite of the poverty and lack of material possessions, Cambodians are remarkably image-conscious. My usual uniform for school is a pair of Crocs, a shirt, and a black skirt. My students do not like my Crocs, my headbands, or the gym shorts I wear when I teach PE. I know; they tell me.

"Ms. Bo, you got even fatter over weekend."

I try to explain that that is rude, but it really isn't rude to them. They call each other "fat," "chunky," and "ugly," too. Not much is verbally taboo with them. American taboos such as a woman's age, weight, or appearance don't exist here.

My first time at the "fancy" grocery store with imported items left me stunned. I was looking for some simple face lotion in the beauty product aisle. Out of the ten lotions there, nine of them were whitening creams. Women here want so be white like the Western women they see on TV. These bleaching lotions promise to make them look like American beauties. Women avoid the sun, not for health or comfort, but to avoid getting darker. "Whiter is better," or so they tell me.

And because I am white, I am stared at all the time. When I ride my bike to school, motos will nearly crash as the drivers try to turn around to examine me, the foreigner. On the street people do double takes. People are always staring at me. Sometimes I feel like a caged animal. Groups of people will see me a half mile down the road and continue staring at me the entire three to four minutes until I am out of sight. Sometimes they are silent, but most of the time they are not. Sometimes I know what they are saying.

People take pictures of me or capture the "walking white girl" on their video phones. It is so hard not to feel unwelcome and frustrated by all of this. I don't look like them, talk like them, or live like them. No matter how comfortable I may get here, I will always be the "foreigner." It feels awful knowing that I will never just blend in. I can't.

Considering all of this, I compare it to life back home. When I see a "strange" person, do I take pictures of them, stare, or laugh as they walk by? Of course not. That is rude and inappropriate in the States. Did you catch the keywords, "in the States"? Both cultures think alike—we know we see something strange—but our reactions differ.

Americans look away; Cambodians just keep on looking.

CHAPTER 22

HWJT?
(How Would Jesus Teach?)

"Don't be in any rush to become a teacher, my friends. Teaching is highly responsible work. Teachers are held to the strictest standards. And none of us is perfectly qualified. We get it wrong nearly every time we open our mouths."
—James 3:1, 2

God continues to lead the way, and I keep praying the big three. I pray every day that God will help me to leave this eating disorder in Cambodia, that I will find a friend or some community, and that God will show me my purpose. I keep praying and God keeps working.

My eating disorder is becoming less and less a part of my daily life. A year ago, I didn't have a daily life. My life was living with an eating disorder, and I could focus on little else. I counted every calorie that entered my mouth, I would never leave the house without looking perfect, and workouts were long, hard, and painful.

I still endure plenty of difficult days and irrational moments trying to counsel my way through this, but I see improvement. Now, I am more likely to forgive myself, I talk more kindly to myself, and food and exercise are less of my focus each day. Somehow I am picking up the missing pieces as I continue to recover. I can't live the way I have been. I was created for so much more.

I am still praying for friendships and community, and I am trying to do my part. I keep myself busy and try to plan activities with people. I spend time with the Scotts, go to the riverside with JC, or socialize with a young group of teachers who just graduated from Mission College in Thailand.

Lastly, I am not only praying for purpose but I am praying that God will help me see that this is worth it. I want Him to show me what I am supposed to do here. But I also want Him to show me that it matters to someone, anyone. I know this is a tall order, but God hasn't given up on me yet.

Last week I wrote in my journal: "So since God is showing me that ED and other things are not my purpose, what is? Am I *actively seeking my purpose* or just waiting around for conditions to be ideal? As I seek my purpose here, I wonder, how would Jesus teach my classes? What would He do differently?"

Jesus, the true Super Teacher, would not get so frustrated when students forget to call him Mr. Jesus. He would not get so annoyed with the eleventh graders' complaints and requests. Would Jesus give out the death glares I do to Ratana in seventh grade? Doubtful. I'll bet Jesus would make more time for those catty girls in eighth grade. Jesus would be a little more merciful and patient than I am day to day.

After really evaluating my teaching goals in the light of Jesus' character, the week seems to go much better. I am more intentional. I don't yell. I talk quietly to students one at a time. I smile when I want to put my hands around their throats and . . . whoops! Never mind.

As I try desperately to control and maintain order in my seventh grade classroom, I try to imagine Jesus smiling happily from the back of my classroom. He is smiling because these are His children—they just might not know Him yet.

CHAPTER 23

Super Teacher

*"No test or temptation that comes your way is beyond the
course of what others have had to face. All you need to remember is
that God will never let you down; he'll never let you be pushed past
your limit; he'll always be there to help you come through it."*
—*1 Corinthians 10:13*

Heather, why did you come to Cambodia?" Fay asks me through my tears. Just when I think I have it all together, I fall back into old habits and ways of thinking. Frustrated with my classes, frustrated with my living situation, still lonely, tired of battling this eating disorder and needing a shoulder to cry on, I am back on Fay's couch.

"Well," I sniff, "I wanted a change of scenery from college, and I've wanted to be an SM ever since I was a little girl. I wanted to do something that mattered and to experience a different way of life."

"Do you even enjoy teaching?" she asks matter-of-factly.

I hesitate. Good question. Some days I really don't like teaching at all. Some days I dread it. This really gets me to thinking. What do I dislike so much about teaching? What makes me wake up so often and think, *Why in the world am I still here?*

I think about my chaotic seventh graders. Most of them are really good and sweet and smart, but I spend so much time chasing around the "bad" kids and Ratana with ADHD that I don't enjoy my time with them. The classroom can get so crazy that sometimes I leave in tears. I try not to let them see me because that would mean they have won. Unfortunately, most days I walk out of my classroom feeling like a failure as a teacher, knowing that Jesus would never treat those kids the way I do.

I think about my eighth graders. I spend so much time enforcing my "No Khmer" rule that I'm not even getting to know them. The girls are afraid of me, the boys sense I am miserable, and they probably dread class as much as I do. Sometimes I will just glance at the students and they will state defensively, "We were speaking English!" I hate feeling as if I am little more than a guilty conscience to them.

I think about my tenth and eleventh graders. They are only a few years younger than I am, and they know it. Some of them speak very good English and correct my grammar. One particular student named David challenges me in class, and I've been proven wrong before. All in all, my high school students are intimidating, and I feel like a fraud every time I stand before them. They deserve better.

After talking with Fay and thinking about the specific reasons I dread teaching, I know if nothing changes I will definitely not survive all year. Once again, it's back to the drawing board as I examine my attitude and behavior toward my students. It's time to tweak things a bit more.

In seventh grade I start laughing at the ridiculous things Ratana does. The other day, he just stood up in the middle of class and yelled, "I feel so good!"

I didn't encourage him to continue yelling, but I kindly asked if he would sit down so that we could continue. The girls in that class are so sweet, and I have been intentional about praising them for being such good students. I'm noticing that as I give the good kids more attention the ornery boys are getting jealous.

In eighth grade I am trying to go easier on my stricter standards. Before, if someone was blatantly speaking Khmer, I would speak firmly, "Puthereak, English, please!" Now, I give them fair warning, and if they keep it up, they have to dance and sing the Macarena for all of us after class. If that doesn't work, I chase them around and pinch them. I started eating lunch with the girls at their desks and getting to know them one on one. We gossip, we talk about the boys, and we learn more about each other every day.

The high school students are still an adjustment. How do I instantly stop feeling intimidated by 64 eyeballs staring me down each day? I talked with Fay and the principal about the intimidation factor. They basically told me that my age should not matter. I have important insights to share, and they need to listen. I need to approach them with the same confidence and authority I do with the younger kids.

The days are becoming easier now that I believe that I have something important to tell them and there is no way all of my students are going to love me. Yesterday in class David corrected me on my past participle use of the word "run." I didn't even know what a past participle was until I read about it last week.

He kept asking me more questions. I told him I would be happy to help him after class, so he came later and asked away. I admitted that I didn't know the answer to all of his questions but I would be happy to look for the answers.

I am far from a super teacher. I don't breeze through the days. I haven't discovered the magic solution of teaching, but the days are less hectic and a little more peaceful. More purpose and less hopelessness. That's a good sign. Who knows? I may even *enjoy* teaching someday.

CHAPTER 24

End of the Rope

*"You're blessed when you're at the end of your rope. With less of you there is
more of God and his rule. You're blessed when you feel you've lost what is most
dear to you. Only then can you be embraced by the One most dear to you."*
—Matthew 5:3, 4

On any given day I love and hate Cambodia all in the same breath. I still
long for home, often, but is home really what I need? If I went home
today, would I be satisfied or am I making it out to be something it isn't?
Would I really fit in back home after the past four life-changing months? I
promised God this year of my life, yet I am having a really hard time handing
it over.

In Micah 7:7-10 it says: "But me, I'm not giving up. I'm sticking around
to see what God will do. I'm waiting for God to make things right. I'm
counting on God to listen to me. Don't, enemy, crow over me. I'm down,
but I'm not out. I'm sitting in the dark right now, but God is my light. . . .
But it's not forever. He's on my side and is going to get me out of this. He'll
turn on the lights and show me his ways. I'll see the whole picture and how
right he is."

I'm not ignorant to the probability that I will appreciate this experience
years from now. True, I may forget just how much it hurt and even advise
others to be student missionaries themselves. But right now, I'm in the present, and the question still remains: *How do I get through tomorrow?*

This morning I read Matthew 5:3, 4. These words jumped out at me: *end
of your rope, lost,* and *embraced.*

Yes, I feel as if I have been living the last four months at the *end of my rope.*
Yes, I feel as if I have *lost* what is most dear to me: my relationships, my family,
my sense of self, perspective, peace, etc., etc.

But do I feel *embraced*? No. Will I see how God has worked this year—

will He "turn on the lights"—only when it is all over? Am I ungrateful and oblivious to how much God has been working in my life already? God has brought me this far, hasn't He? God has a spotless track record. He hasn't let me down yet. Where do I get the nerve to doubt?

Eating disorders are the most deadly of all mental illnesses. Yet, I'm still alive and kicking. I'm still here.

Tomorrow is coming whether I like it or not. I'm doing the best I can. I'm living as balanced a life as I can for where I am. I am not promising perfection, but God doesn't require it anyway.

CHAPTER 25

Wishes

"A wish is a desire without energy."
—*Paramanhansa Yogananda*

My parents will be here in 13 days. I wish I felt ready for them to come. I wish I could show them the great life I have made for myself here. I wish I could have them meet tons of new friends. I wish I could show them what a fabulous teacher I am. I wish I felt stable. I wish I could show them that I am doing all right and that they don't need to worry.

I wish. I wish. I wish.

I guess it is what it is. Reality isn't going to change just because my parents are coming into town. I suppose I had just hoped that by this point I would be all settled in and adjusted, and I would truly be living the "student missionary experience"—whatever that means. In my mind I'm not sure I will ever be living the SM experience because being an SM with an eating disorder sounds like such an oxymoron to me. My struggles remain. Aren't godly missionaries supposed to have it together enough to avoid mental illnesses?

Sometimes I get e-mails from a really sweet girl from Union College who is working at Maxwell Academy in Africa. She sends pictures of her safari adventures, she tells stories about how much she loves her job, and she has a great support community that takes good care of her. I am painfully envious. Interestingly, Maxwell Academy was my first choice when I wanted to be an SM. But for some reason, it didn't work out.

On Monday I talked with my eating disorder counselor, Teresa, on the phone. We've spoken only twice since I have been here, but I need her to help me get my head back on straight. Before I left, my parents and I made a deal: if at any point Teresa said I needed to come home, I would. I promised to be completely honest with Teresa.

"It's been an awful last two weeks," I told her. "Since Thanksgiving I've started binging on anything and everything to try to make myself feel better, even temporarily."

"Heather, what are you willing to sacrifice to stay in Cambodia? Is this really worth it?" she asks me.

"Fighting this all alone is wearing on me. But some days I feel like my pride is the only thing keeping me here. I think, 'I can't go home. I will be the SM who came home early, the SM who failed.'"

"You've been giving and giving since you got there. You have been desperately trying to reach out to people, hoping to make friends. You have been giving so much energy to your students every day. You have been volunteering, trying to get involved. But you rarely get anything back. Of course you are lonely."

Because I don't have many meaningful relationships here, I feel a void. I have been using food to try to fill that void, so I have binged every night for the past two weeks. Binging is painful and not something I like writing about.

My coping weapon of choice is food. Other people choose alcohol, drugs, cutting, shopping, gambling, or pornography. We all reach for something to help us cope when life hurts too much. Each day leaves me feeling hopeless, pathetic, disgusting, out of control, and more lonely than I did before. I have very little left to give to others when I am so selfishly concerned about myself. This is just what the devil wants, and lately it seems like he is winning.

Yesterday I told someone that I came to Cambodia all alone. He quickly and optimistically responded, "Well, no you didn't. You came with God! Put your chin up." He grinned and walked away.

Well, thank you for that! I wanted to smack him, but he's bigger than me.

Yes, I do have God. On most days, He carries—yes, carries—me through my day. My loneliness has forced me to rely more on God. But many mornings I wake up and say, "God, enough is enough. I just can't do this anymore. I need friendship."

During our conversation Teresa told me to make a list of what I had *hoped* to accomplish in Cambodia and another list of what I *have* accomplished in Cambodia. After completing the assignment, I examine the lists. They are quite different. I have so much to do here. There is so much I came here to do and haven't been doing.

I add the lists to my growing assortment of writings. I don't write because it is fun for me. Most of the time, writing is painful, and I wonder deep down if I have lost some people's respect as a result. The bottom line is that I am trying to be honest in my writings.

My friend Sandy made me think about what God meant when He said in the Ten Commandments, "Do not lie." Did He really mean that when someone asks "How are you?" you should only report on the pretty parts of life? Could that same commandment be read, "Be completely honest"? I'm not saying God wants us to mope around spilling our guts to everyone we meet. But as far as I have experienced, I have very little to lose by being transparent with people. I won't lie about my situation here—the good, the bad, and the foreign.

As I struggle with my wishes and desires, there is hope. The Scotts have offered to let me live with them after the Christmas break. I feel hope knowing that my parents are coming soon and I will be moving into a more nurturing environment.

I am eager to see my parents, to hug them, to talk with them, to poke them and make sure they are real. I want to show them how I live and prove that I am not embellishing all of this. I wish for their input, their suggestions, and their point of view.

In 13 days.

CHAPTER 26

"This Really Is Chaos!"

"Out of clutter, find simplicity. From discord, find harmony.
In the middle of difficulty lies opportunity."
—*Albert Einstein*

What will they think? How will they react? Will they think I have been exaggerating the last four months?

Anxiously, I stand waiting to pick up my parents from the airport in Phnom Penh. I shuffle back and forth and stand on my toes. I'm eagerly waiting for the first time I'll see my parents in four months, which feels like four years.

I keep thinking, *There they are*, but I'm wrong over and over again. Finally, two familiar faces emerge. They scan the teeming crowd thoroughly until they see me and smile with relief.

Beaming and bright-eyed, I envelop them in desperate arms. I hold them for a long while before letting go, much like a life preserver in a bad storm.

I thought I'd be unable to hold myself together, but I'm OK. We hug and just stare at each other for a while, unsure if this is really happening. We load up and head to Tim and Fay's where they will be staying.

It's surprising how quickly we go back to "normal" in an entirely abnormal situation. We are now in Cambodia, the country I've been describing to them through e-mail. Now they can see it with their own eyes.

By the riverside, they have their first meal in Cambodia, which ironically is Mexican food. I usually can't afford this restaurant at five dollars a plate, so it is their treat. We take a tuk-tuk, which is a trailer with seats pulled by a motorbike.

Anxiety overwhelms my parents' faces as we pull out into the chaotic traffic that I've grown accustomed to by now. Coughing at the dust that threatens to choke them, they cover their mouths and try to rub the dirt out of their watering eyes. I watch their reaction to the trash heaps along the side of the road. Begging children tug at my dad's shirt and plead for food to eat. I see his eyes fill with tears. He realizes there is nothing easy about this. It just isn't right.

"Wow, honey, this is intense! Now all of your e-mails make sense. This really is chaos," my mom yells over the honking horns as we continue down the road.

"Yeah, it's a lot to take in, huh?" I respond somewhat sarcastically, enjoying every minute of their reaction to my reality here in Cambodia. "It feels so good to see this through your eyes. It makes me feel a little less crazy!"

Dad assures me, "Oh no, we believe you. But we fully understand now that we've seen it for ourselves."

The next day I take them to the market where I buy my produce. It is crazy and smelly; they walk around with their mouths open. Raw meat sits covered with flies and squirming fish wait to be beheaded. I reach for my regular fruits and veggies. I have to admit that it is fun to watch their reactions.

"Heather, are you sure this is safe, ya know, to eat?" asks my dad.

"No."

After a day in the marketplace, I bring my parents with me to school. My kids have been anxiously awaiting their arrival. The previous week they had asked lots of questions.

"Your mom beautiful like you?"

"She is more beautiful than I am," I said.

"Wow!"

"They rich, your parents? Your father, he give me money for a helicopter?"

Now my students are able to meet my parents in person, and they love my parents. As my parents take in all of the sights and sounds—the heat and stickiness, the huts, the flies, the construction site next door, and the screaming children—I can tell that they are overwhelmed. I am glad that my parents are getting the picture of what daily life is like for me in Cambodia.

On Friday there are no real classes since it is the last day of school before Christmas break. Instead, we have our own Christmas "parties," which means that the kids have more free time and less study time. Although Cambodians do not really celebrate Christmas, the kids like the parties because they know that this is what Americans do.

During worship with my eighth graders, my dad pipes up, "So who is the fastest student in this class?"

About four scrawny, mischievous boys proudly jump out of their seats. Everyone is giggling.

"OK, so do you think you are faster than me?"

"Aww, yeah! I could beat you. You are old!" quips Vanny.

"All right, let's go see."

My dad leads them in a dramatic precursor to the big race. He bends over and touches his toes, stands up and twists his arms from left to right. After a convincing warm-up, the racers are ready.

A line of ten boys and one Khmer teacher are ready to race this crazy American.

"I'll take the first two racers," he says. "We'll start here and run to the end of this path." The finish line lies about 50 yards away."

I jump in. "Wait, wait! Let me go to the end to see who wins."

I've seen my dad run, and I've seen these kids run. Dad is really fast, but he's also 54 years old. Surely my vivacious eighth graders can beat him to the finish.

I yell, "On your mark, get set, go!"

As my dad and the two boys bolt toward me, it is apparent how this race will end. I'm so proud as my dad passes the finish line seconds ahead of the others.

"No way!" Vitya immediately appears to humiliate the boys. "You too slow! Mr. Bohlender so fast, no chance for you!"

The remaining racers forfeit in disbelief, and the story is told and retold all day.

Later that day we enjoy the Christmas program. The parents were invited, but few actually come. The idea of supporting the kids at things like this still hasn't caught on.

Each class shuffles nervously onto the stage. One by one, they sing a song or play recorders and quickly shuffle off.

Each year the finale to the program is the nativity story acted out in a Christmas play. My tenth grade class has been collecting costumes, building a wooden shelter, and painting pictures of barn animals for the last two months.

As with most other performances, not everything is perfect—a few barn animals tip over in the wind; Mary says, "I look silly holding this doll!" and tosses it on the floor; and the wise men make up their own script—but once it is all over, I'm relieved and they are happy.

CHAPTER 27

Assurance

*"Each one of these people of faith died not yet having in
hand what was promised, but still believing. How did they do it?
They saw it way off in the distance, waved their greeting, and accepted
the fact that they were transients in this world. People who live this way
make it plain that they are looking for their true home. If they were homesick
for the old country, they could have gone back any time they wanted.
But they were after a far better country than that—heaven country."*
—*Hebrews 11:13-16*

Since it is Christmas break and I do not have to teach, my parents and I
fly to Bangkok, Thailand, for a few days. It amazes me how different Thailand is compared to Cambodia, even though we are only an hour away from
my home.

It is weird to see a modern airport, not be stared at, drive on the left side
of the road, drive on a highway going 70 miles per hour, and have drivers
stay in their lanes! I spot a Starbucks and a McDonald's. I'm not necessarily
craving these foods, but it is comforting to see familiar landmarks.

Bangkok is still crazy, but it is "organized" chaos. There is some order here,
unlike Phnom Penh, which is completely out of control and basically shuts
down at 6:30 p.m. because everyone is scared to go outside.

We wander our way through wats, or temples, that are speckled with Buddhas everywhere we turn. Mom has come armed with her *Lonely Planet*
guidebook, so we have a general idea of where we are. She knows the streets
of Bangkok surprisingly well. For all I care, we could've been locked up in
a closet together for 10 days and I honestly would've been thrilled. Really.

We spend some time in Bangkok as well as the gorgeous island of Koh
Chang. We soak up several nights at a resort: beautiful, peaceful, clean, and
spacious. Hallelujah for room to breathe! We swim in the ocean, sit by the

pool, ride elephants through the jungle, take lots of pictures, and talk and talk and talk. We never run out of things to talk about. I find myself thinking, *OK, so peace does still exist.*

"Ya know, sweetie, you can come home," my dad says. "We won't think any less of you. You've done well, and if it's just time to come home, that's OK."

"I know I can," I respond. "But I feel stronger after seeing you guys, and moving in with the Scotts could be a lot better. I have to try."

Apparently it is Christmas day, although it sure doesn't feel like it. Coming from the cold, snowy winters of Colorado, Christmas at a beach in Asia is a new one for me. Having my parents, the two most influential people in my life, sitting beside me is the best present I could have received this year.

My parents' visit provides me with, in a word, assurance. Assurance that I am still the same girl that left home a few months ago. Assurance that this is temporary and it will not last forever. Assurance that I have total support and coming home would not be the end of the world. Assurance that, while this is hard, I am strong and can do this. I want the same confidence they have in me. I want to be proud of me too.

I leave my parents at Bangkok International Airport. They are catching their flight back to the United States while I am flying back to Cambodia. We fight the tears while trying to smile and stay optimistic.

"Six months is nothing, right? Maybe it will just fly by," says Mom, trying mostly to console herself.

"Yeah, OK. See ya soon." I walk away. *Why am I doing this again?*

Leaving them isn't any easier the second time around. The only thing that has changed is the airport and country.

Blood-spattered Concrete

"God told them, "I've never quit loving you and never will.
Expect love, love, and more love! And so now I'll start over with you
and build you up again, dear virgin Israel. You'll resume your singing,
grabbing tambourines and joining the dance."
—*Jeremiah 31:3, 4*

Cambodia feels a little different to me now. Mostly, as a result of seeing my parents, I've been able to gain some new perspective. Upon arriving back in Cambodia, I move in with Tim and Fay. Hoping for a little more space and added companionship, I look forward to the change. Now I actually have a place to be alone with God. So I take advantage of it, get ready for the day, and leave at about 6:30 a.m. for school.

After a full day at school I jump on my bright-red mountain bike, don my face mask to keep out the dust and pollution, and brave the traffic. As I'm riding home, I come upon a large crowd that has gathered in the middle of the street. They are huddling around a boy. Thrashing and confused, he lies bleeding on the ground. Dirt from the road is stuck to the gash in his cracked skull. Rocks are embedded in his knuckles and elbows from the impact of his fall. Thirty or so Cambodians stand around his twisted body as the sun beats down on us.

"Does anyone here speak English? Do any of you know what happened?" I ask.

Blank stares and disinterest meet my request.

Of course, I can guess what has happened: another motorbike accident. I've witnessed the aftermath of at least a dozen crashes since I've been here. This is old news to the locals as well. Their disinterest shows that this is just another ordinary day.

Shouting and murmurs surround me as I kneel beside the teenage boy lying in front of me. Sweat trickles down my back. Traffic continues on the busy road as impatient drivers angrily honk their horns and yell in our direction.

"We need to move him to the side of the road. Do you understand what I'm saying?"

I use hand gestures by pointing at six boys, imitating a lifting motion, and pointing to the edge of the road. They seem to understand as they move in closer to grab a limb. I lift up his shoulders, but his head starts to fall back as the rest of his body rises. I quickly reach out my hand to support his bloody head.

Together we move him out of harm's way as onlookers laugh and chat curiously.

Scarlet blood coats my hands. "Here, use this," a Cambodian woman offers me a wet wipe.

"Oh, you speak English. Do you know what happened?" I ask quickly.

"I don't know," she says, pointing to his motorbike lying on its side. "The people are saying that another bike came, hit him, and then took off."

"Can you help me? We need to call someone for help. Are there ambulances?"

"I don't know." She looks confused.

"Is there someone who helps people when they get into accidents on the road?"

"I don't know. I'm sorry. I don't understand," she replies wearily.

The boy on the ground opens and closes his eyes and tries to get up several times. I firmly press down on his shoulders, trying to explain that he needs to lie still. I ask another woman to get him some water and something to prop his head up so that it is off of the germ-infested ground.

I am not a nurse. I am not a doctor. My only medical experience is a first aid class in Pathfinders. The only thing I remember is the importance of keeping him still in case he has neck or spinal injuries. So, that's what I do.

Cambodian children watch me with keen interest as I just sit there, unable to communicate with them but unwilling to walk away either. I keep hoping someone has gone to find help.

Blood streams from his head through the dirt. Putting his hand to his head, he sees the blood, and alarm sweeps over him as he proceeds to shift around and mumble again.

At this point I contemplate running to the mission down the street where I can possibly get some help, but I worry about what the people will do while I am gone. I have never realized that basic first aid is such a distinction of higher education. I thought everyone knew this stuff.

Over the murmurs and discomfort of everyone's stares, I detect a high-pitched siren. A massive weight lifts off of my shoulders. I may not have to sit here and watch this boy die, feeling responsible that I couldn't do anything.

The noise grows closer and louder, and indeed, an ambulance has come for him. What a relief!

A few Cambodian men hop out of the truck and wordlessly lift the boy into the back of it. Shutting the gate, they load up and drive away.

I just stand there for a while. The observers walk away. Children go back to their games and everyone returns to their lives like any other ordinary day. I am left standing with dirty hands, blood-spattered concrete, and perspective.

Just another day in Cambodia, I suppose, but not to me. I will never know how the accident happened, what they were all yelling about, or if he is even alive.

CHAPTER 29

Weapons

"God will defeat your enemies who attack you.
They'll come at you on one road and run away on seven roads."
—Deuteronomy 28:7

Early morning is my new time to exercise. It's refreshing to be out in the cool air, and it helps me start my day off right. This morning I am up at 4:30 a.m. for my walk before school.

Groggily, I make my way down the stone stairs to the front door. I lace up my tennis shoes and drink some water. It is dark outside except for the eerie orange glow from the streetlights.

I insert only one headphone so that I can hear what's going on around me. I grab my can of pepper spray that reads "Protector of Mem [sic] and Women." My dad bought it for me in Thailand. Sounds trustworthy, right?

I place my key in the padlock and lock it behind me. I hold the keys in my left hand, one key jutting out between each finger of my clenched fist. With pepper spray in my right hand, makeshift brass knuckles in my left hand, one headphone in, and running shoes on, I'm ready to go.

As I walk toward the main gate of the compound that leads onto the street, the guard startles me. He sleeps upright in a chair every night. He looks at me, unsurprised, and rolls his head back to go to sleep.

I tiptoe past him toward the main gate.

The gatekeeper, a small humble man with big ears, hears me rattling the metal gate as I try to get out. He emerges from the guard stand where he was sleeping and says "Oh, sorry. I unlock for you."

"Thank you," I whisper, a little sorry to be waking him up for my morning jog.

He lets me out onto the street.

A woman with a veil over her head slowly rolls her cart down the street in my direction. She doesn't make eye contact. She is collecting recyclables, hoping to get them before anyone else.

The darkest portion of my trip is directly in front of the compound where I live. So, with pepper spray raised before I round each corner, I finally make it onto the well-lit main street.

Five or six other exercisers are already out at this time. A few Chinese foreigners power walk up and down the street. Everyone carries a three- to four-foot-long stick. They say it's to keep the dogs away.

Excited by the opportunity to be in public without getting a lot of attention, I start my walk up the street and turn left, away from the compound. It is still pretty dark at 4:45 a.m., but plenty of people are already awake, building fires and cooking rice.

This road is a little darker than the last one I was on, and I wonder if I should turn around, but I'm already halfway down it. I decide to keep going, walk to the end, and go back toward the mission compound.

Slight creaks and whistles make me walk a little faster, and I catch movement to my right. *What was I thinking coming out at this hour?*

Ah yes, I remember. Eating one spoonful too much guarantees a workout the next morning. A side effect of my eating disorder is compulsive exercising. I feel fat and anxious if I don't get in my daily workout. But as I walk this morning, I wonder what might happen because of my illness.

After several minutes of walking through the dark, I reach the end of the road and head toward home.

The lights are getting brighter as I come out of the shadows. Shacks along the way house Khmers starting another day. A few meander outside and sit, watching as I walk by.

Keeping a hurried pace, I spot a teenage boy to my left on the other side of the road. He is leaning up against a wall, staring at his feet. I steer farther to the right side, completely turn off my already low music, and clench my fists.

I try not to make eye contact, but am totally aware of his presence out of the corner of my eye. My heart beats a little harder as he slowly looks in my direction and straightens up.

I pretend not to notice, but he moves to block the road where I am headed. I look him in the eye, and for the 500th time, I wish I could speak Khmer. About 15 years old with dark hair and dark eyes, he looks like most Cambodian teenagers.

I veer to avoid him, but he stands erect and confident in the middle of my path. I start to walk to his left; he shifts his feet. I try to walk around him to his right; he moves there as well. He raises his hands in front of him in a cupping motion as if asking for help. I let my guard down slightly and look him kindly in the eyes, trying to figure out what he wants.

He looks me right in the eyes, quickly drops one of his hands, and grabs for my crotch. He pushes his hand between my legs. I immediately jump back in disgust and disbelief.

"No. Aw-tay!" I say, flustered. "Very bad."

He steps toward me again mimicking my words. "Aw-tay! Aw-tay!" He laughs and smirks at me. I try to hurry past him down the road. Curses in English rain down on me as I try to get away.

Mind racing and eyes wide, I quicken my pace and look around to see if anyone is watching. Tears stream from my eyes as I look for a friendly face, but there are none. I quickly head toward the next brightest street light, fearfully peering over my shoulder.

I instantly remember all the warnings I've grown up hearing about what to do if you are sexually assaulted, but none of them seem to fit my scenario. Images of family and friends flood my mind.

I'm suddenly conscious of the "weapons" in my hand, but they don't seem nearly as threatening as they did 20 minutes ago when I left home.

Is he alone? Does he have a weapon? How am I going to make it home? I hear his footsteps, walking, no, running behind me.

Still shocked that this is happening to me, I whip around, pepper spray raised high. I am fearful of what he will do next, but I have to act now. He screeches to a halt a few feet away.

Obviously pleased by the tears and terror on my face, yet curious about the black spray can in my hand, he smirks and continues laughing. This is a sick game, and he is enjoying the power he holds over me right now. I am the foreigner in his country, on his turf, and there is nothing I can do.

Sternly, I say, "Aw-tay! No. Go home!" as I point behind him.

He just keeps smiling at me and laughing happily. He steps toward me, testing my limits. Now, slowly backpedaling away from him, I get ready to run if I need to.

He doesn't step any farther but just stands there with his eyes locked on mine, a mischievous grin on his face. He seems a bit less confident with the presence of the pepper spray in my hand. I slowly take a few steps backward and turn around, hoping he doesn't follow me.

A group of Chinese walkers is coming down the road in my direction. I've never been so glad to see complete strangers. I continue walking quickly in their direction, but I still sense him about 20 feet behind me, taunting me. Relieved to be around people, I half walk, half run my way home to safety.

Why is it that the very people I came here to help are the ones making me feel the least wanted? It isn't fair to speak for all Cambodians, but it is hard to step outside of the house or outside of the school. I don't feel safe, especially not after this incident, and I'm tired of them taking pictures, glaring, pointing, staring, laughing, and making jokes.

What causes people to be so cruel? What did that boy accomplish by attacking me? Was he out for sexual satisfaction or just out to scare a foreigner?

I was paralyzed the rest of the day at school, imagining that every Cambodian boy I came in contact with hated me and wanted to hurt me. After my obvious attitude shift toward the boys in my classes, I realized that the teenager who assaulted me was winning by leaving me scared.

Love is, and always will be, my ultimate weapon. I have to fight through the pain and fear and love like Jesus loved. Of course, as always, knowing what you should do and doing it are two totally different things.

CHAPTER 30

The Red-light District

"The point is not to just get by. We want to live well,
but our foremost efforts should be to help others live well."
—1 Corinthians 10:23, 24

Claustrophobia pounds me often in Phnom Penh. I hunger for open space and room to breathe. Desperate to see something green, JC and I head east on his moto toward the massive and muddy Mekong River.

We pass over the Japanese friendship bridge and onto the other side: heading away from Phnom Penh. Humid air saturates me, coating me with anything that sticks: bugs, dirt, and who knows what else.

JC tends to drive pretty fast, so on top of the humidity and the wind, my already big, curly hair gets even bigger. Even on the edges of town there are still people, motos, and buildings cluttering every inch, but there is a little less traffic, and there is actually open space where we can catch glimpses of the sunset. Once in awhile we catch whiffs of unpolluted air. *Ahh, so nice.*

I don't always know what to say to JC. We come from such different places. Usually our conversations revolve around my many questions about Cambodia.

I tell him about being groped the other day. He doesn't seem surprised. As I tell him about it, I realize I am kind of fishing for an apology.

Why? JC didn't grope me, but a Cambodian did, and JC is Cambodian. That's not fair to him or to anyone, but I have a hard time seeing each person as separate when overall the culture really wears on me. I suppose that's the essence of prejudice.

Sometimes I wonder if he really understands half of what I say. The other day, he showed me a badminton racquet that cost $240, and I whistled in that way we, as Americans, do when something is big or expensive. It starts high and slides low, as if to say, "Wow! That's expensive!"

He just looked at me like, "Why are you whistling?"

My students had the same reaction the other day when I said, "You guys are really on the ball!"

They looked at me blankly and said, "What ball?"

Sarcasm is lost on English learners, so that eliminates about 25 percent of what I have to say.

After driving for a while, we stop at what you might call a carnival. It's open every night of the year and maybe a hundred people gather there. It consists of 15 game booths of the exact same game and the exact same prizes! You'd think that someone would say, "Hey, what if my booth offered a different game?"

So, we throw darts at balloons because that is all there is to do. The prizes include dirty stuffed animals, cans of beer, and bottles of dish soap. What a pity that neither of us won. (See, who would I be without sarcasm?)

After playing a few games, we move to the center area where the food is sold. Cambodian "restaurants" do not have roofs, walls, chairs, or tables. Instead, there are hammocks, bamboo mats, a blaring big-screen TV playing a Khmer comedy, and very questionable food.

Respecting my vegetarianism, JC orders some corn on the cob and papaya salad, which is in sharp contrast to what everyone around us is eating—half-grown chicks out of the egg, frogs, and fish balls on a stick. I realize I must be adjusting, because none of this fazes me anymore. I am dirty, there are naked children brushing up against me, I can't understand anyone, most people are staring at me, and I definitely encounter "something" not vegetarian in my papaya salad, yet I take it in stride.

We eventually head home. On our way we drive through the red-light district, famous for its prostitutes, drunken fights, and crime. This is where the men go for paid sex.

I ask, "How do you know there are prostitutes here? I don't see any."

"You can just tell," JC says. "They stand outside the wooden shacks with the neon lights inside."

He begins pointing out the girls to me. But after a few I can recognize them without his help. They don't wear particularly scandalous clothing or signs that say, "I'm a prostitute." They don't have to. I can tell by the look in their eyes.

Their eyes tell stories of exhaustion, defeat, and worthlessness. The girls are all about 18 or younger. It is difficult to look at them after awhile. They aren't talking or laughing with each other. They are just sitting with fear in their eyes, waiting.

"JC, what would happen if I walked up and offered one of those girls a job instead of prostitution?" I ask.

"I don't know. I think some of them like what they do."

"I don't believe you," I answer strongly. "You're telling me that these girls enjoy being sold for sex every night? Do you really believe that?"

Still mostly uninterested, JC repeats, "I don't know. I think some of them like what they do."

"I can't believe that. I'm sure maybe some started doing it because of desperation for money, but others are forced into it. Maybe I just want to believe that if offered something else, they'd take it."

As I get ready for bed, I can't stop thinking about those girls. I keep wondering what goes through their minds. I wish I knew what they were feeling. I wish there was some way I could talk to them. I want to better understand how they got where they are and what life is like for them. I can't get their faces out of my mind, and I'm not sure I want to.

I crawl into bed surrounded by my "things" and think, *How did I get it so good? Why am I so blessed?*

My mind continues thinking about my life versus their lives. *What's the point of coming to Cambodia, living and experiencing it, and then going home and pretending it doesn't exist?*

I've stopped viewing the luxuries of my life here as mere luxuries. They are distractions. Air-conditioning helps me pretend it isn't sweltering hot outside. I live in a safe, clean, and supportive home with the Scotts, pretending like it isn't dangerous, dirty, and unwelcoming outside. I listen to my iPod when I walk the streets, pretending I don't feel the loneliness and isolation of being a foreigner in another country. I read books and watch movies with friends on the weekends to whisk myself away to a better place, if even temporarily, to help forget.

Back home my distractions are different, but just as destructive. I live in America, pretending there isn't a pain-filled world out there in desperate need of help. It's easier that way; it doesn't hurt so much.

The people here cannot afford the luxuries I have. So they live without them. They live in the heat, the corruption, the filth, and the chaos, and they will continue to do so long after I am gone.

I can't stop thinking, *What's the point?* I wonder if the Cambodian people's less-than-friendly reaction to me comes in part from this fact: I am just another white person. I am just another girl who comes, sees, leaves, and might never come back.

Do *they* feel like the circus freaks? Did I come here just to make myself feel better? Because if I just leave, knowing full well that this country won't heal itself, why did I come at all?

Am I only willing to be a missionary for 1/90th of my life (assuming I live to be 90 years old)? I am not saying missionaries live only in foreign countries. There is work to do everywhere. Am I willing to reach out to people and look upon them as Jesus did? Am I willing to sacrifice for someone else? Am I willing to have the spirit of a true missionary no matter where I am?

These are not prideful words or thoughts from an SM feeling like a saint. This is a plea from a human being feeling confused, desperate, and frustrated with herself. My questions arise from seeing the hopeless eyes of the girls in the red-light district and the eyes of Cambodians everywhere.

Nothing seems good enough in such an awful, broken place.

CHAPTER 31

Silence That Hurts

"An honest life shows respect for God; a degenerate life is a slap in his face."
—*Proverbs 14:2*

Thursday morning I find a little kindergarten girl squatting in the showers going to the bathroom. Nearly dumbfounded, I point to the shower and say, "No."

I take her by the hand and lead her to the toilet and say, "Yes."

She looks at me like, "Yeah, have you tried climbing up on that thing?"

In Cambodia we have a lot of squat pots that actually flush. In India, where this little girl is from, they just have a hole in the ground. Her reasoning makes sense. The shower drain probably looked much more familiar to her than the huge porcelain monster.

Later, I am sitting in the back of my eleventh grade morality class listening as Navy teaches the lesson. Suddenly, from the front row, Leckanah screams and shakes violently. I look to the other students. They don't look very surprised, but they stand up curiously.

She is crying and lying on the ground squirming. With my mouth open, stunned and unable to move, I wrack my brain trying to figure out what is going on.

Gasping for breath, she takes deep sobs. I ask Leeta, "What is going on?"

"Oh, Leckanah is angry."

"Angry?" I repeat to ensure I am hearing correctly.

"Yes, she is just frustrated," she answers, as if that somehow explains why Leckanah is on the ground screaming.

Like good friends, the other nine girls are by her side, rubbing her ears, fanning her face, massaging her legs, and talking rapidly in Khmer. By the look of it, she could've been giving birth. The only two boys sit in their seats, watching the commotion, completely uninterested in the whole thing.

"OK, girls, back off for a minute. Leckanah, I need you to take a deep breath with me. You need to breathe" I tell her.

She continues hyperventilating. The girls crowd back around her.

I'm thinking she might just be enjoying the attention. "Girls, give her some room!" As Leckanah continues thrashing and crying, I scoop up all 105 pounds of her bony frame and make my way to Fay in the library.

A trail of girls follows me. As I make my way up the stairs, I tell the concerned girls to return to class. Entering the library, I plop the high school junior on the library pillows. Gladly, Fay takes charge.

Apparently these outbreaks aren't terribly uncommon here. I witness them at different levels: tempers, complete silence and refusal to talk, physical violence, and more.

Cambodian culture says, "Suck it up and move on," so Cambodians stuff it all inside. They don't talk about how they are really feeling. They don't admit when they are having a rough day. They don't want to talk about it. They don't want to disappoint anyone. So they pack it inside until it comes bursting out in different ways.

I have often thought about the mental health of Cambodians since arriving here. Cambodia has had a brutal and horrendous past, but virtually no one talks about it, and if they do they chuckle their way through. Cambodians watched their families murdered; they watched their children starve to death; they watched their own bodies seemingly dissolve.

The Khmer Rouge was Asia's version of Hitler's Nazi army. The dictator was called Pol Pot. He wanted to create a perfect race by eliminating all the smart, gifted, and Western-influenced people. The death toll ranges from 2 to 4 million people between 1975 and 1979. Unfortunately, the killing didn't officially end until 1998, more than two decades later.

Postgenocide there were no group counseling sessions. There was no moral support, national apologies, immediate international aid, support, nothing. So they moved on. They stepped over the dead bodies in the streets; they washed the blood off their clothes and went back to work.

In 1999 after the Columbine massacre in Littleton, Colorado, when two students opened fire on their high school, parents had access to grief counselors and pastors and any other support they needed. That was after Columbine, not after 2 million human lives were extinguished.

HIS-4

As I watch Leckanah's exhausting episode, I am reminded of my own a few months ago, when on my way to school one day, I just could not stop crying. I was hyperventilating, scared, homesick, and in pain. I cried and cried because I had no one to talk to. I needed a friend.

So, for a moment I sense that maybe I understand what Leckanah is feeling.

Whether it is culture or otherwise, silence isn't helping anyone. The problem is that some people deal with stress more violently than with just tears. They rape, they steal, they murder; they are trying to cope.

I leave the library and prepare to give the chapel talk to the high school students. My tenth grade drama class wrote a skit about being honest. This is a perfect opportunity to talk about honestly sharing your feelings.

"What does the commandment mean that says, 'Don't lie'?"

Some answers come from the group. "It means, tell the truth."

"So, if someone asks you how you are doing and you say 'fine,' but you aren't really 'fine,' are you lying?"

They hesitate, but all of them agree that that isn't being completely honest. Still, I doubt any of them are thinking, *Hmmm, maybe it is OK to be human and admit when I am having a bad day!* It seems to be a culture thing. I doubt it will click that easily. It didn't for me and continues to test me.

"An honest life shows respect for God; a degenerate life is a slap in His face" (Proverbs 14:2).

I haven't studied all that the Bible has to say about lying, but so far the biggest and greatest changes in my life have come from living a completely honest life, as difficult as it may be. Honesty with the people I love, honesty with God in heaven, and honesty with myself.

Honesty continues to save and liberate me, but watching my kids carry around their burdens in secret is painful. This is all they know.

CHAPTER 32

A Fly on the Wall

"The moment you think you understand a great work of art, it's dead for you."
—Oscar Wilde

Good morning, Ms. Bo!" the students chime together as I step onto the crowded bus.

A few boys joke, "You can sit with me, teacher!"

I load into the red CAS bus filled with 22 excited seniors. I am one of five sponsors going along on the senior class trip to the ADRA adventure camp.

I take a place in the front to avoid motion sickness, which is multiplied by 10 on Cambodian roads. We depart after prayer and the journey begins.

Maybe my senior year is just too far in the past, but I never remember being so noisy, and I'm almost positive we weren't. Khmers have only one volume level: loud.

There are some extremely musical seniors in this class, and one of them just bought a new drum set. So, of course, the full trap set has a seat on the bus as well. Also, along for the trip are two guitars, a recorder, a harmonica, and some vocal, energetic students. We will spend about eight hours in the bus together with no air conditioning, no room to breathe, and enough floating dirt in the air to fill a sandbox.

Two hours into our trip we get a flat tire and pull over in the little town of Skun. This village has the nickname of Spiderville because they specialize in large, fried spiders.

We spend some quality time together in the heat while they fix *two* tires that have gone flat. Three hours later, we are on our way again. Next, we stop in Kompoung Thom for lunch. I am already sick from the ride, so I don't eat much.

From here we have four hours to go and those hours are spent on a dirt road pocked with what Americans would call "craters." I'm not exaggerating. Some "dips" go down four feet before we barrel up the other side. The bus rumbles on as the students continue screeching, singing, and banging on the bass drum.

After a few hours I ask, "Umm, can we please pull over for a minute? I'm going to throw up."

The bus driver obviously doesn't know what "throw up" means, so I act it out, and he immediately slams on the brakes. Thanks.

Continuing farther into the less populated countryside, we finally arrive at the ADRA adventure camp, staffed by seven Cambodians who run the activities and cook for us.

We divide boys and girls into cabin-type bungalows. They are just wooden shacks with pads to sleep on and mosquito netting. I take five girls with me and we go to bathe. Oh, if there were only showers! No, here we use dip showers.

Being naked is a big no-no in the Khmer culture, even with the same sex. So I put on a krahma, a full-bodied sarong, and follow the girls. There are two large cement troughs filled with cold, brown water and a few plastic dippers. I watch and follow.

Each girl squats next to the trough in her krahma and starts dumping the water on her head. Bathing with clothes on is quite difficult; I never feel completely clean, but it's better than nothing. By nighttime I am exhausted and glad to have some quiet. Sleep comes easily.

Apparently one shower is not enough, and my girls are up at 5:00 a.m. to bathe again. The whole camp is awake. I pass on the second opportunity to dump dirty water on my head and lay thinking, *Why, oh why, must they get up and start yelling this early?* About this time the drums start, too. That wicked trap set. Even so, I feel surprisingly rested and head down to the picnic/kitchen area for breakfast, which is vegetarian and solves a lot of my usual problems.

After breakfast, we start with worship and then the ADRA workers lead us through the day to different activities. We do all kinds of group games: blind walk, rappelling, a zip line 600 meters long, trust fall, and so much more.

Everything is extremely well organized, keeping the kids busy and interested all day long. There are a lot of challenges that involve critical thinking, communication, and working together. It's fun to watch them struggle through the challenges. I probably miss a lot of the experience because they tend to slip back into speaking Khmer, and my translator keeps forgetting about me. But that is to be expected. It is also forcing me to learn some Khmer just to understand what is going on.

Later in the week, we hike a little ways and camp outside. We build a campfire, roast sweet potatoes, and sleep in hammocks. The next morning we are all very sore and a bit grumpy. Hammocks are far from comfortable for me, and sleeping with the bugs and critters isn't relaxing either.

After a fun-filled week, we prepare to leave. Unfortunately, we get away late, and of course, the bus gets another flat tire. Halfway into the trip, we stop for lunch. Little did we know that a few miles down the road our brakes would go out in the middle of nowhere. It's approaching dark, and we still have four hours to go until we reach Phnom Penh.

"So, any ideas about what we are going to do?" I ask the bus driver.

He just chuckles and says, "Oh, it's going to be OK!"

"Well, I'm sure it's going to be OK, but, see, I have a plane to catch in the morning. I'm going to Malaysia, and I really don't want to miss it."

He puts his hand up in the air, and within 30 seconds a bus stops. He says, "Here you go. You can take this to Phnom Penh."

Still shocked at his seemingly magical powers, I numbly gather my things and climb onto the other bus.

I start to question this decision when I board the bus full of Khmers and realize I cannot communicate with anyone and am still reasonably far from home. A few young men look at me and then at each other and snicker excitedly. I try to avoid eye contact as much as possible. I sit there thinking, *Wow, it could be a really long time before anyone would realize I was missing!* This is probably not my best decision.

Four hours later I arrive in Phnom Penh after dark. As we pull over to stop, the moto drivers run alongside the buses to pick up weary travelers and take them wherever they need to go. A few drivers peer inside, point at me, lick their lips, and blow kisses my way. I pick the oldest, weakest-looking one that I imagine I can defend myself against if I need to. Gratefully, I find that he gets me home without any problems.

I return to an empty house, start my laundry for my next trip, take a shower, and eventually fall asleep.

Other than the headache I acquired from being surrounded by 22 very loud Khmers, I really enjoyed the trip. I will never forget it. I realize that I thoroughly enjoy any opportunity to be with people here and not stick out like a dislocated thumb. The kids are used to my "whiteness" and "foreign-ness" by now, so I just get to *be* me. I often wish I could be Cambodian for a day just to better understand what goes through their minds. I want to be an unobserved fly on the wall.

I was also reminded how greatly I miss the outdoors, the trees, and fresh air. I got to "rock climb" up a huge rubber tree at least a hundred feet high and rappel my way back down; the closest to mountains this Colorado girl is going to get for a while.

CHAPTER 33

Chinese New Year

"Believe those who are seeking the truth. Doubt those who find it."
—Andre Gide

"I'm waiting in the dark. I'm crying all alone.
I'm watching for a sign. But so far you haven't shown.
I've tried to save myself. I've done all I can do.
And so my last resort, I finally look to You.
How did I get to here? Jesus, hold me near.

"I'm so tired of my self-seeking salvation; turns out
I'm so much smaller than I thought.
I was sick of playing "savior"
Then I realized, you never asked me to.
Maybe I'm not that strong.
Maybe you are what I needed, all along.

"I'm waiting in the dark. I've set myself aside.
I'm ready to be changed. Lord take away my pride.
Still living with the pain. Still trying to get through.
How can I be so blind? This is also hurting You.
How did I get to here? Jesus, hold me near."

Exactly a year ago I wrote this song. I wish I could report improvement, but I don't feel it. The words were true to me then; they still are. So after a year has passed, why don't I feel better? I'm still fighting the same demons every day. I have been living with this eating disorder for nearly two years. Amidst different opinions on the topic, some say I'll never fully recover.

Today I'm at the Koh Ching Seventh-day Adventist Church in Malaysia. As

I sit through a dry, uninspiring sermon, I cannot turn off my restless mind. I keep thinking about how redundant church has become. The more non-Christians I talk to, the more their reasoning makes sense. Doesn't the idea of Christianity seem kind of hokey sometimes? Maybe it only appears silly to me because I haven't truly experienced God for myself, whatever that means.

Last night I chatted on the computer with my brother-in-law, Ben, one of the wisest people I know. I was telling him about a book I just finished reading. *Appointment in Jerusalem* is about a Danish woman who prayed to see Jesus for herself, promising that if she did, she would follow Him the rest of her life. She opened her eyes and the image of Jesus was standing in front of her. She asked for signs; she got them. She needed money to survive; she got it. She needed answers; she got them.

"So, Ben, if this woman prayed and got the answers she wanted, why doesn't that happen to me?" I asked, not really expecting an answer. I continued typing, "What's wrong with me? I've been working hard and pleading with God to give me some relief in Cambodia and from my eating disorder. Yet, I don't hear a sound."

He responded after a while, "Heather, what would happen if you prayed for a sign from God and didn't get it?"

"I wouldn't be surprised," I answered. "I never actually expect my prayers to make it to God."

Maybe that's the problem. I've never truly believed God hears me. I wonder if I am approaching an agnostic belief system because I think God exists only for super-Christians and prophets.

Sure, I can speak Adventist lingo—words like salvation, forgiveness, Sabbath, communion, haystacks, *The Desire of Ages*, and Second Coming. I've had 20 years of practice. But what do I believe?

My thoughts return to my current surroundings. I've been in Malaysia for a week. I flew here with Dina, a teacher from school, and her husband, Chheangley, for the Chinese New Year celebrations, when everyone goes home to be with their families. Chinese New Year is the equivalent of Christmas for Americans.

We arrived Friday and stayed in Kuala Lumpur, or KL. Now it is Sabbath, and we are attending one of the many Adventist churches in KL. The entire congregation is Chinese.

There are three main people groups in Malaysia: Malays, Chinese, and Indians. Also scattered in there is a large African community and many Iraqis. But there is only one religion: Islam. If you are born in Malaysia, you are Muslim. Period. If you convert to another religion, you are thrown in jail, or worse.

After church I find myself visiting with a group of church members. Curious about the religious atmosphere in the community, I start to ask some questions. "If the laws in Malaysia are so stringent, is there any opportunity for witnessing or outreach?"

Laughter pours from the church members like an overflowing bathtub.

"Oh, no," one member informed me, "if we are caught witnessing to a Muslim, they could kill us. The laws are in place to restrict all religious influence besides those that are Muslim."

After the effects of my silly remark die down, the room falls silent and I notice how much this sad fact of life really weighs on them. No one really wants to talk about it. Fear dominates their lives. They cannot freely share their beliefs. The next day we head to Dina's hometown; Koh Ching is on the island of Borneo in the state of Sarawak in the country of Malaysia. Quite a geography lesson!

I really like Dina's family. Her mom, dad, and 12-year-old brother welcome me with full Chinese hospitality. Everything is performed quickly and spoken quickly, usually in very high decibels.

The next four days I spend enjoying the Chinese New Year traditions. All the family gets together at the eldest family member's home. Dina's grandparents had eight children, and in turn, these children made more babies, swelling the family to more than 30. So, in their humble home, we cram in for the festivities, which mostly include eating, watching TV, and playing a game called mahjong, or Chinese dominoes.

Mostly it is chaos, but they are happy. I obviously don't know anyone, but they all quickly take to calling me Nicole Kidman because of my curly hair. I assure them that they are weirdly confused.

New Year's Eve includes a large feast of mostly meat. They are embarrassed to find I am vegetarian.

"How do you survive without eating meat?"

Eating meat, especially pork, is so important in the Chinese culture. So becoming a Chinese-Adventist and not eating meat is, to them, almost like my burning the American flag. Well, maybe not quite so extreme, but either way, it is very important. The night is rounded out beyond midnight as fire-crackers explode all around us.

Splashes of red paper litter the ground the next morning. The following 15 days of celebrations go like this: every morning extended family visits the grand-parents and they eat. Then, they visit distant relatives they haven't seen since last Chinese New Year and eat. Then they visit this uncle and that uncle and eat some more. They all joke that the 15 days of celebrations should be followed by 15 days of fasting, because that literally sums up the holiday.

I don't understand the Chinese all around me, so I talk to the kids. We practice their English by playing a guessing game.

I say, "OK, it is red on the outside and white on the inside and you eat it! What am I?"

"An apple!" they chorus. "More, more!"

"I am brown and fluffy and say, 'Meow.' What am I?"

They cheer excitedly, "A cat!"

We play this game for hours as we visit house after house. Jasmine, a "6-almost-7"-year-old gets the most excited, hopping around in dramatic, an-imated movements.

She looks directly at my red bag sitting next to me and says, "OK, guess this one. It is big and red and you carry things in it. What am I?"

After awhile, the game gets old, but sudoku does too, so playing with the kids is a nice break.

Chinese New Year is about being close and relaxing with family. It is a tra-dition that spans nearly 4,000 years.

My time in Malaysia ends too quickly, and I am sad to report that I didn't really see much of the country. I wanted to see the beach or the zoo or some local character. But I suppose enjoying Chinese New Year firsthand with a Chinese family was quite an experience too.

Being surrounded by this family has left me more homesick than ever. The feeling of loneliness remains as I struggle with being the subject of conver-sations, stares, and awkward whispers. I like to think they must believe I really *am* Nicole Kidman and just can't believe their eyes.

Happy New Year, Nicole.

Cambodia Adventist
Church, located
on the mission
compound where I lived.

Above: Angkor Wat is Cambodia's most famous temple complex.

Left: Giant banyan trees at Angkor Wat.

Above: During the late 1970s the Khmer Rouge led a genocide against Cambodia, killing millions of people.

These are pictures taken before they were murdered.

Above: Two-story-high tower of human skulls at the Killing Fields, one of the largest killing and burial sites of the genocide.

Left: The Killing Fields.

Left: The market where I would buy my fruits and veggies.

Right: A moto, or motor bike, is a great way to get around for one person. A tuk tuk is a larger cart that's pulled by a moto and works better for two or more people.

Left: That's me, with Liz (center) and Trina (right), volunteers from W Walla University.

Right: Ms. Bo's school rules got a bit beat up with time.

Below: Ornery eighth grade boys.

Ms Bo' Rules
Clean Room
-trash
-uniform
-furniture.
Happy Room
-be respectful
-be kind
Safe Room
-no stealing
-no hurting others

5 days!

We might have been learning the macarena in geography.

Left: Tim and Fay Scott, my family/support/ sounding board/prayer warriors in Cambodia.

Right: JC and I head out on his moto.

My friends from Mission College (from left to right): JC, Chheangley, Dina, Sockha, and Angie.

A traditional Khmer dance presentation.

Mmmm! Deep-fried spiders!

My fearless friend, Polly.

The amazing tenth-grade class.

Hanging out in tenth-grade English class

Fay Scott. What a gem!

Left: Eleventh-grade students playing Catch Phrase, a surprisingly effective method of learning vocabulary words.

Riding to the Khmer New Year celebration.

Feisty eleventh-grade gals—always a good time!

Cambodia Adventist School.

The new school that's being built behind the existing school.

Traffic on the road never ceases.

We do not have elephants in our parks back home!

CHAPTER 34

Never Enough

"Be thankful for what you have; you'll end up having more.
If you concentrate on what you don't have, you will never, ever have enough."
—Oprah Winfrey

Heather, I can only judge off of your e-mails, but it sounds to me like you are depressed."

My cousin Angie, a counselor, helps open my eyes to harsh facts of life sometimes. I don't want to admit it, but I agree with her.

"Oh great, another mental illness to add to the list. What should I do?"

We talk about what it means to be depressed and how I need to change my perspective and situation as much as possible.

Angie sends me a book in the mail and it helps me learn about what depression is and how to heal from it. Reading the book reminds me that we all hold core beliefs in our lives. Some are true, some aren't. For those of us that live by false truths we've been telling ourselves for years, reality just gets in the way.

For years I've been telling myself, *You are not enough.* Thus, I am an overachiever. I am never smart enough, involved enough, organized enough, friendly enough, sporty enough, pretty enough, or as I decided two years ago, skinny enough. When I tell myself that I am not enough, any small setback seems to be a huge failure.

I need to make some changes. I came here to find God, but I feel farther away from Him than ever. Of course, it's hard to find something you are not looking for. Guilty.

I keep praying, if you can call it that. I am begging for answers to my three big prayer requests—recovery from ED, purpose, and friends—that I was praying for a few months ago. Unfortunately, my prayer time usually turns into a nagging session about the things God is *not* doing for me.

So I need to make time for God. This week I've been getting up at 4:00 a.m. to spend a good hour reading my Bible and praying. I struggle with the fact that I can speak the Christian lingo but I don't actually know God for myself. I can preach a lovely sermon on almost any topic, but I don't know what it feels like to fully rely on God and trust that He will carry me through. So with every verse I read, I ask myself, *What is this teaching me about who God is?*

At the end of every day I finish this sentence as many ways as possible, "I am glad I woke up this morning because…" This has completely changed my perspective because some days I have to search really hard for things to put on the list.

So for this week, "I'm glad I woke up this morning…"

-for the funny Chinese man waddling down the street flapping his arms like a bird

-to begin to trust God with my anxiety

-to laugh and play with Vitya in eighth grade

-get an Oprah magazine in the mail

-to dance and sing with the eleventh graders at worship

-to book tickets for my trip to Australia in April

-to meet an American teacher named Polly who teaches at a local Christian school

-to get my second Christmas package in the mail from Union College

In the midst of my attempt to praise God for another day, I have to deal with the realization that I think I have worms. Apparently, it is really common here. Either way, it seems that I've been sick and miserable for several months now. I hope taking some pills will help.

Fay tells me, "Yeah, I remember when an SM got worms in Africa. She didn't know she had them until they were crawling out her nose! But, I'm sure you'll be different."

"Why are you telling me this?" I exclaim.

"Just thought I would share. I guess I'm immune. Sorry hon. We'll get you some pills. You'll be OK."

Easy for her to say.

CHAPTER 35

Tim and Fay Scott

"We make a living by what we get, we make a life by what we give."
—*Winston Churchill*

Let me introduce you to the two greatest people in Cambodia: Tim and Fay Scott.

Tim and Fay are in their 50s or 60s. They have been missionaries in the field for more than 20 years. They have two daughters who came along for some of their adventures.

They started in Alaska before going to Hawaii and then Africa. Their daughters grew up overseas, and then attended college in the States. Tim and Fay moved on to Egypt and then here to Cambodia. They are two amazing human beings. I've said it before, and I will say it until the day I die: if it were not for Tim and Fay Scott, I would not still be here.

Tim and Fay are my parents here. We can sit together in silence, or we can jabber endlessly about nothing at all. I love it when they tell me about their mission stories: getting robbed three times in Kenya; getting a throwing star chucked at Tim in the dark; difficult people; difficult places; interesting food; and less-than-ideal living arrangements. Many of their stories start with, "Oh Tim, remember that one time we were traveling across Africa…," to which I usually reply, "I wish I could start my sentences that way!"

They've been married 35 years, and they are perfect for each other. Fay is the talker, and Tim is agreeable and easygoing. She scurries around the house, and Tim sits and reads a book—besides he'd probably just get in her way.

Today Tim is home at lunchtime. Fay comes in and squeals, "Look, Mr. Tim is home! Hi!" She hugs him from behind and holds him for awhile. They grin at each other.

I'm actually convinced these two people love one another. They have been through so much together: different countries, faith-testing trials, needy SM's like me, and much more. They've been to places where all they had was each other for entertainment, support, and even the same language.

Fay jokes about getting old: "You know, maybe it is just because I am getting old, but the traffic today was awful!" Tim and Fay's daily stresses would send most average Americans their age to the emergency room.

I usually try to remind her, "What you go through day to day is far from normal. Please, give yourself a break."

They are a healthy couple, good Christians, and people everyone comes to for advice. I'm so blessed to live with them.

I get to wake up in the morning to Fay's beautiful and cheerful smile, "Good morning, dear, how'd you sleep?"

I like Fay. She smiles when she talks. She laughs. She listens. She does what she can and leaves the rest in the hands of God.

Tim isn't such a morning person, but he's never unpleasant. So usually Fay and I chat as if so much has changed since we both went to bed eight hours before. We share duties such as washing dishes, filtering water, locking all the doors and windows, and eating leftovers.

Speaking of food, Fay hates, loathes, dreads cooking. She jokes that Tim knows his way around a kitchen because it was what he had to do to survive all these years. Fay knows her way around a kitchen, but she would just rather not spend much time there. Friday afternoons we usually cook together to share the load. I talk about my grandpa, my little cousins, my memories growing up, and traditions from home. Other times we talk about how crazy Cambodia is and how crazy we are for living here.

Tonight I made some weird tofu/quiche/casserole/mush thing. Bless their hearts. Tim just said, "Food is food, and at least Fay didn't have to endure the cooking process!" Poor souls. They ate happily and never once complained.

The Scotts do not understand that they are far from normal. They are extraordinary. I don't know how to help them understand how important they are to me. I try to pull my weight around the house. I try to listen and be attentive when they talk. I try to give them their space and peace and quiet as much as possible. I cook for them whenever I have time. I put the toilet lid down, because Fay admits it's a pet peeve.

Since moving in with the Scotts about two months ago, much has changed. My burden of depression has lightened. I binge far less frequently. I've started doing yoga again. My prayers and time with God have been more intentional and genuine. I laugh much more and cry much less. I enjoy teaching more than I have all year. I have more energy to play.

I randomly tell the Scotts, "Have I thanked you yet this week for allowing me to live with you?" If the Scotts had said "no" to letting me move in with them back in January, I would be in Colorado right now. But here I sit on a Friday night, Sabbath candle flickering.

I'm not ready to settle down in Phnom Penh, Cambodia—I am far from in love with my location—but I am falling hard for the people. I realize that I want to see my kids graduate. I want to see whom they marry. Will Chamrong and Somphos from tenth grade ever hook up, or does he really like Phalkun? I may never know. I want to see if my eighth grader Vitya becomes Cambodia's next prime minister, because if anyone does, it will be him. However, I worry about him because he talks often about bombing other countries. He's a slightly aggressive individual.

I want to see the day when Navy from eleventh grade speaks confidently in English and does great things with her life. I want to see Pen David become a pastor and change this country for the better. But I can't.

I should've seen this coming. These incredible people have really snuck up on me, and I don't want to think about leaving them.

The other night I couldn't sleep, so I wrote a poem. I wrote it about all the Cambodian people here and how their life differs, yet relates, to ours.

WAITING
Sitting, standing, waiting,
Statues on the street,
They take their place every day,
People I long to meet.

They watch me as I pass them by,
Their eyes so hard to tell,
I want to know the thoughts inside
That tired-looking shell.

Their stares are full of questions
And thoughts they can't express,
So as I round the corner
Again, I feel so helpless.

Every morning I see them,
And this is where they'll stay,
Until the sun has tread its path
Through yet another day.

Not sitting in anticipation,
For the arrival of a friend,
But sitting just to pass the time,
Waiting for its end.

Isn't it so pointless?
Have they nothing better to do?
Is there purpose in their lives?
Are they just waiting till it's through?

Waiting for something better,
Waiting for hope to fill
Those long-deserted places,
That reality tends to kill.

Is there something I am missing?
Or something I can't see?
Until I live one day like them
It will always be foreign to me.

But home is more familiar
And things are different there;
We do things on purpose
And without a minute to spare.

Yes, we fill our day with "things,"
Tasks, priorities, and such;
But when we close our eyes at night
Does it really amount to much?

Aren't we just waiting at our jobs
And waiting our way through school?
Waiting to feel wanted
When the world is being cruel?

Aren't we waiting through entertainment
To distract from what's outside?
Aren't we waiting in distractions
To avoid the things we hide?

Aren't we all waiting for something,
The hope of so much more?
The dream that it was worth it,
The "This is what life's for!"

We are sitting, standing, waiting,
Statues in the world.
Our postures may be different:
Same destiny unfurled.

The differences seem vast
But no one wants to be alone.
One thing we have in common:
We're all just waiting to go home.

CHAPTER 36

Desperation

*"Where's the strength to keep my hopes up? What future do I
have to keep me going? Do you think I have nerves of steel?
Do you think I'm made of iron? Do you think I can pull myself up
by my bootstraps? Why, I don't even have any boots!"*
—Job 6:11-13

I've always had my questions about God. I can think of very specific
times in my life when I either felt incredibly close to God or incredibly
distant.

I felt incredibly close to God my sophomore year at Campion Academy. I
had a series of seven surgeries during my time in high school. The procedures
were for several things, the main problem being a benign tumor growing
inside my ear canal. Now, I am mostly deaf in my left ear.

Honestly, at one point I thought I was going to die. I've never felt such
agonizing pain or felt so humbled to realize that I had no control over my
life. I felt so powerless I couldn't help realizing "something" was keeping
me alive, and it wasn't me. I went on a youth retreat to the beautiful mountains of Colorado. I felt God there.

I felt incredibly close to God when I attended a Christian church on Friday nights, where the worship was honest and raw and real. I saw God differently than ever before.

As I mentioned, I've also felt distant from God. I felt far from God when
my cousin Jake died of cancer. How do such tragic things happen without
reason or justice? He was a young firefighter and single father to a bouncy,
red-headed, 6-year-old daughter. I didn't understand why or how, so I was
just mad, mostly at God.

I felt horribly far from God when the eating disorder took center stage in
my life. I didn't have time for God. I was too concerned with myself. ED is

an incredibly selfish disease. There isn't room for life goals or silly things like "purpose." Not much else mattered but me.

I remember last year, my freshman year at Union, driving home with my sister and telling her that I had purged a few nights before. I sobbed uncontrollably. It was raining hard, and I shouldn't have been driving because I could hardly see. I felt so guilty, ashamed, disgusting, unlovable, and hopeless. The weeks and months that followed that night were spent just trying to put the pieces back together and possibly believe that God could ever love me. I didn't see how, but I was told that He did.

I've never felt farther from God than I have the past six months when I first came to Cambodia. Aren't I the strangest, most oxymoronic student missionary you've ever heard of? I am in a foreign country labeled as a "missionary," yet I am questioning my beliefs in God, and I continue to fight an eating disorder that dominates my thoughts more than I'd like to admit.

The past few days I've been reading through my journals from high school up to now. It seems I've been battling the same self-defeating thoughts and questions about God most of my life. I feel stuck. From almost two years ago, when I was first told I had an eating disorder, up to now, I've hardly moved. The same thoughts, same struggles, same mere existence permeate my days.

Deep down I know that I have moved forward, but it seems so slow. Two years ago I fully believed that my "only" worth in life depended on my appearance. Two years ago I counted every calorie that entered my mouth. And in its place I ran long and hard, even with arthritis in my knees. If I ate more than the amount I had decided on that day, I took care of it in whatever way necessary.

I'm not in that place anymore, but my current situation doesn't feel much better. Tonight, I plead desperately with God to heal me. I gasp my way through several minutes of inability to form words. When I can talk, the words for a prayer just don't come, so I keep sobbing instead.

Looking at the ceiling, I wonder, *Why do I believe in God? This is ridiculous. This is probably the greatest conspiracy in the world's history.*

Through a whisper, finally the words come. "God, I'm begging you, show Yourself to me. I just need one sign."

I stop and listen. The tears slow, and I lie silently, afraid to speak. But I don't hear anything.

Crawling into bed, I turn off the light. Another uneventful night without answers. Isn't the SM experience supposed to bring me closer to God? I feel more filled with doubt than ever before.

If God does not audibly or physically show Himself to us, then what are we supposed to be hanging on to? I don't want to believe in a God that I am supposed to see only in happy little children, the sunrise, or the breath in my body. When can I hug Him? When will He *actually* wipe the tears from my eyes? If the breath in my body is our only proof of a loving God, then I suppose He'll have to kill me for me to understand. And I guess that sort of defeats the purpose, right?

Is the whole idea of reading the Bible so that we learn how God thinks, so that we learn to answer our own prayers? Sure, it is much more hopeful to believe that there is something bigger and greater in control of everything. I want to live with hope, but what if we are wrong?

I also despise the argument of, "Well, if we are wrong in the end, what did we lose? At least we lived with hope!" I don't want to live only with hope; I want to live with proof. I want to believe in something that makes sense.

Maybe I just don't know enough about the Bible. Maybe I haven't done my homework. Maybe I still have so, so much to learn. God didn't say our lives would be easy, but He said we'd never walk alone, right? Sorry, I feel alone.

Yes, I have the Scotts. Great people. I'm glad. But does God *really* use people or is that just a lie to get people to believe in God. "Yeah, there's a God. He works through people." Whoever invented that argument was smart because, of course, there will always be people to prove that there is a God, *if* there is a God.

Here in Cambodia, spirituality must be self-sufficient. There are no youth groups, no inspiring speakers, no weekend retreats, and no deep conversations about God. I am empty, empty. But shouldn't I be able to maintain a spiritual life without those things? Because if I only had a spiritual life "with" those things, then what is my spiritual life really about, anyway?

Do I have this all wrong? Am I making up a God that doesn't even exist? Please help me understand if I am. I just feel very confused about who God is.

I haven't turned cynical, but I am critical. I am convinced that God doesn't want mindless, numb robots. I think He wants to be chosen and believed in because of what we know, not what we've been told. Questions are not evil; they lead to understanding. I just want to understand.

I guess I'm tired of counseling myself. I mean, come on, I am "reading" my way out of depression and trying to "think" and "talk" myself out of an eating disorder. Now I am trying to answer all of my own questions about God. I'm tired of comforting myself. I am tired of wrapping my arms around myself and saying, "Ssshhhh, ssshhhh, it's OK. It's going to be OK. Try again tomorrow. It will be OK."

I continue to get up in the morning and read the Bible as I search for answers. I continue to pray at 4:30 a.m. I haven't given up. I just don't understand, and I am desperate, desperate for a reason to believe, again.

CHAPTER 37

Twenty-three Questions

"Courage is fear that has said its prayers."
—*Dorothy Bernard*

I am living in fear. Some days I feel like I am just waiting to get hit by a car or get in a moto accident. Other days I anticipate getting groped or worse. I actually imagine the exhaust filling my lungs and giving me lung cancer, which is incredibly common among the locals here. I live in the fear that I will never blend in, and standing out scares me.

"God hath not given us the spirit of fear; but of power, and of love, and of a sound mind" (2 Timothy 1:7, KJV). So that should just solve all of my problems, right? What am I missing?

Today, in the middle of the afternoon a man walking in my direction reached out to grab me, and I had to run to get away from him. He was no doubt just trying to get a rise out of the "white girl" and make his friends laugh. I walked away whispering, "Don't cry. Do not cry. He cannot make you hate him if you don't want to." No, these people can't make me hate them. But it sure feels like they are trying really hard.

I tell my students about it.

"Oh, Ms. Bo, the boys stare and grab at you because you are beautiful. Don't be mad."

I am little more than a sexual object to the men here. Foreigners have been kidnapped and locked away in hotel rooms with men for several days. The men lick their lips and make kissing sounds at me as they stand holding their infant children in their arms. I just don't understand.

So, no, God has not "given" me a spirit of fear. But does that mean I can't be scared? Yes, God is powerful. Yes, God is love. If I really believed, would that be enough? I guess I just don't have enough faith.

Is my fear and hurt standing between myself and the work I came here to do? I am not the first person in the world being asked to love the unlovable. How do some missionaries thrive while I continue to be paralyzed? Is this all really easy and I am just horribly weak?

"Heather, what do you think God is trying to teach you in all of this?" Fay asks me.

I can't answer.

I am not oblivious that God is trying to teach me *something*. But I have never felt as distant from God as I do right now. I am used to being spiritually fed. I come from the college life where people acquire "Jesus points" by attending vespers, chapel, and so on. There is no shortage of spiritual activities to go to. I am used to having God served to me. I hate writing that, but it is true.

I have no such programs or community here. Do I really have the spiritual life I thought I did? Or did my relationship with God revolve solely around meeting Him at the next vespers, singing at the next nursing home, and sitting through the next Sabbath school?

No, I didn't sign up to save prostitutes. All I have to do is teach my English classes each day and I will have fulfilled my purpose, right? After all, that's what I said I would do.

It doesn't seem good enough anymore. I see the needs of the people here. But it is proving difficult to serve a culture I am increasingly afraid of. Is there just a missionary "type," and I am not it? Maybe I am simply not strong enough for this? Did I misread the signs? When I prayed for God to show me where to go, did I really listen long enough? Did I stop to listen at all?

I do not enjoy talking about God's will. No matter the conversation, there never seems to be a resolution. I always receive a watered-down answer. How do we know God's will? Are our very lives God's will? Were each of these keystrokes predicted thousands of years ago? Or does God let us decide? He has the best way that He hopes we will take, but in the end is it up to us?

I don't get it. It is easy for me to say, "Well, you prayed for an answer and now you are in Cambodia, so that must be God's will." That's silly. I could pray that I not stub my toe all day. Then, I stub my toe and say, "Whoops, I guess that was God's will."

I suppose I shouldn't be talking. My last prayer was probably, "God, when will all of this be over? What do You want from me? I don't get it!"

I don't want to come home a bitter person who claims that this has been the absolute worst year of her life. But this week Fay told me, "Maybe you are just trying too hard. This picture of 'super SM' you came here with just isn't realistic."

Super SM loves everyone. And while I wish I could, I'm just not there yet. I wish I were, but I am not.

Am I unfairly assuming most Cambodians are self-satisfied in their ignorance? Some are; that has been proven. But how do I reach those who desperately need and want the help I came here to give?

I am asking a lot of questions. Twenty-three questions to be exact—I counted. But all are rhetorical.

I have never had the prayer life I wish I did. So, I can't make any promises. But I am determined that if God is going to move in a big way in my life, I need to start talking to Him about it.

Each weekday morning by 4:00 a.m. I will be intentional about praying. I want to believe. I want to work for God. But I just don't seem to have the strength or the compassion it takes. That's what I'll be praying for too. Each morning I will be praying for strength for another day and an open heart to be able to better love these people.

Chapter 38

Stuffed Animals and Storybooks

"If all of us acted in unison as I act individually there would be no wars and no poverty. I have made myself personally responsible for the fate of every human being who has come my way."
—Anais Nin

My classroom is made up of walls with holes, doors and windows that do not lock, a number of broken desks, and a marker board that is waiting to fall from the wall the next time a soccer ball hits it. Sometimes first graders will poke their heads through the large holes in my wall and screech, "Hello, Ms. Bo!" and run off giggling.

We use blue plastic patio chairs in every classroom. Each break time the students get out, run around, and kick up dust that floats into each classroom and threatens our ability to breathe. I can't leave anything out that smells or tastes good for fear that the family of mice hiding in my desk will get to it before I do.

Every textbook we use is copied because there are no copyright laws in Cambodia, and we can't afford them new. Tattered and falling apart, the condition of the school reflects the condition of the people inside. Worthlessness breeds worthlessness. I see it every day.

There is a mandatory picture of the king of Cambodia in every classroom. He sits on a huge throne, crown and all, wrapped in a luxurious gold and red robe that reaches at least 10 feet behind him. Each day he stares down upon us as a regular reminder to these kids that the king does not care and isn't doing much to help them either.

The mental health in Cambodia is something I think about as often as I change clothes. *How do people live this way? What are they really thinking?* Cambodians often bash themselves and their country. They talk about how stupid Cambodians are, how terrible the crime is, and how Khmers are basically second-class citizens to the rest of the world. Of course they say these things; that's what they've been told their entire lives.

In the States we tell our children, "You can be anything you want to be! Reach for the stars! Dream big. You have purpose. You matter. You can do it. Go for it!"

Well here, the message is, "You are Cambodian and always will be. Don't try to get out of it. You will always be stupid! Your efforts at a better life are pointless! You are stuck. If you leave to get an education, you are deserting your family, and in turn, we will desert you!"

I haven't seen any form of national pride since I got here. Singing the national anthem each morning is more a joke than anything. The kids don't believe the words they are singing, and they don't believe in the country they call home.

Polly, my new friend I met a few weeks ago, invited me to see the school where she teaches. Polly is originally from Pennsylvania, but like myself, she came searching for something more. She teaches kindergarten at Logos, a Christian school that uses an American curriculum. Upon entering, the first thing I notice is order. Surrounded by nicely trimmed grass and trees, the basketball courts teem with energetic players. Classes are taught in real buildings, not huts. A swimming pool sits in the corner of the property. That's right—a swimming pool.

As I wander around, I discover that every class is taught in a clean, nicely decorated, air-conditioned room. Entering Polly's kindergarten classroom, I am shocked by the "childness" of it all: paints, coloring books, a computer, nap mats, cute little desks, bulletin boards, tiled floors, little hooks for their backpacks. It looks like a wonderland in the vast dirtiness of Cambodia.

At CAS the kindergarteners don't have art supplies, stuffed animals, cozy mats to sit on, storybooks, audio books, blocks, anything. They have wooden desks and walls. There is nothing warm, cozy, or orderly about CAS. Jealousy and sadness flood over me like a cold shower. Logos is for the rich Cambodian children and the expatriate and/or missionary kids. CAS is the cheapest nongovernment school in Phnom Penh.

Upon returning home I am unable to figure out why I'm suddenly so sad.

"Almost every time I go to Logos, I feel a little sad that our kids don't have the same things," Fay tells me.

I realize that I feel the same way.

I don't have to teach in air-conditioned rooms where there are hooks for colorful backpacks and a pool, but I feel so sad that I can't give very much to my kids. They have to endure each school day just as I do. They deserve what those kids have, but they'll never get it. They deserve to have textbooks without ripped-out, missing pages and desks without curse words carved into the wood. They deserve a safe place to learn where they can breathe and relax and be kids.

No, a million-dollar establishment does not guarantee happiness. So before you say that maybe my kids are happy where they are, I get it. They may be happy, but it just pains me to see what some kids have and what my kids don't have. Why can't my poor children get the best schooling? Why can't they be driven safely to and from school in BMWs instead of walking several miles in the hot sun?

Right beside CAS is a building that haunts us every day like a bad dream. This is the new Cambodia Adventist School building that has been in the process of being built for several years now and isn't guaranteed to be completed this year either. There just isn't enough money to finish it. They still need thousands of dollars. This hurdle seems so huge; many have just given up.

Still, there are others who keep trying. The principal has started a fundraiser. She has asked every student and faculty member to raise a dollar a day for 100 days. This may not seem like much to you, but here, one dollar could buy lunch and a moto ride home. One dollar is a big deal. So as the teacher, I am supposed to lead my kids in eighth grade to raise $100 each. It is incredibly overwhelming, and I hate asking my kids each morning if they have their dollar for that day, because they never do. They don't have money to give. They hardly have food to eat.

My kids are completely overwhelmed by this fund-raising idea. And while I am trying to be the optimistic teacher who suggests moto washes and selling things, I am fighting years and years of influence much stronger than my own. They've never been told they can do something. They feel so isolated and don't believe that people care that they exist. They've already decided this just can't be done.

The best idea I've had so far is a runathon. They really like the idea because it is easy, and they understand it. I offered to try to raise some money at home. You should have seen the looks on their faces, "You are going to write home to help us? Why would they care? Do you talk about us? Do they know we are here?"

I think that my writing home tells them that I care enough to reach beyond my resources here to do absolutely everything I can to help them. The money I hope to raise will go toward the building project, textbooks, and desks, all the normal school stuff that we just don't have.

In two weeks, I will be organizing CAS's first-ever walk/runathon and will be running in it myself. The plan is to run around the track at CAS for 30 minutes and keep track of each student's laps.

I can guarantee that any money raised will get these kids a better school and a better education. No matter what, I will do everything I can.

CHAPTER 39

The Unlovable

*"Ask yourself what you want people to do for you; then grab
the initiative and do it for them! If you only love the lovable, do you
expect a pat on the back? Run-of-the-mill sinners do that. If you only
help those who help you, do you expect a medal? Garden-variety
sinners do that. If you only give for what you hope to get out of it, do
you think that's charity? The stingiest of pawnbrokers does that."*
—Luke 6:31-34

I've said it before, and I'll say it again. Cambodia equals chaos. I cannot get used to the idea that there are few laws, rules, and definitely no justice. Two 11-year-old girls were raped and murdered last week in Phnom Penh. Without an organized criminal justice system, who knows if the murderer will ever be found? Cambodians have learned, unfortunately, that life must go on.

Moto accidents are common. Robberies are expected. People seek to humiliate foreigners and even nationals. A few months ago a French woman was pulled off her moto while she was cruising down the street. The thief grabbed for the purse around her shoulder, held on cruelly, and dragged her 20 yards until a passing car killed her instantly. All of this creates an environment of fear.

I can't begin to make sense of what I see here day to day. However, I'm trying to accept that I cannot control everything. I need to just let some things go. Take each day as it comes.

This afternoon I sit at the women's Bible study that I am choosing to say God placed in my life. My friend Polly invited me. She enters, looking a bit flustered.

I try to make eye contact with her and whisper, "Polly, are you all right?"

Exhaustion and panic spread across her face as she begins to cry. "I was riding here on my bike, and I looked over my shoulder to cross to the other side of the street. Suddenly, a moto came out of nowhere and hit me from behind!" Her words were hardly understandable as she continued, obviously still shaken. "I flipped over the handlebars onto the concrete."

"Oh no, Polly! Are you hurt?" the women ask.

Wearily she replies, "Umm, I'm walking."

She hit her head, is cut up pretty bad, and is obviously still in shock.

After taking care of Polly, we continue with the Bible study. During prayer requests, I share with the group my questions about God and my difficulties with this culture.

"I've been living here for six months and feel as frustrated as I was my first day! I don't love these people. I am often annoyed by them. I don't feel understood and if there's a God, I don't understand Him either."

Saying it out loud brings more relief than I expected. Several women express similar feelings of isolation and frustration. It feels good to know I am not alone.

"After being groped by that guy a month ago," I continue, "I feel violated, unsafe, and scared around the Khmer people. I'm not enjoying my experience, and I wonder if I should just go home."

Although I feel better knowing I'm not alone with my thoughts and fears, it doesn't take away the questions or provide me with any answers. The ladies don't have any suggestions, but they do provide support.

Thinking back to my morning Bible time, I read, "Satan, who is ever ready to destroy, will, in the absence of love and forgiveness, quickly bring bitterness and division." Well, hook, line, and sinker. Way to go, Satan. You got me on that one.

Yes, I feel resentment and bitterness toward the Khmer people, mostly Khmer men. That makes it awfully hard to love them. It is impossible to love them if I resent them. But loving them hadn't honestly entered my mind until this morning. I figured I was loving them just by tolerating them.

Last week as I was riding my bike home in the rain, a car swiped my hip and hurled me to the ground. I wanted to jump up and scream and yell. I wanted justice. I wanted them to stop and apologize. I wanted them to care, but they kept driving.

This morning a young boy approached me in the dark and kept walking uncomfortably close behind me. I was ready to spray him with Mace. How awful is that? I felt so anxious that I was going to spray a 9-year-old boy.

The Khmers can't make me hate them, but hate is a choice I am struggling not to make. Especially when it seems the whole country is working so hard at it. Thinking about it today, I realize the devil is working hard at it too, one culture clashing with another.

I don't suddenly love all Khmers, but I feel humbled by knowing that, first of all, God loves them just as much as He loves me. And secondly, I am not alone in this. The women in this Bible study are a godsend.

I'm still not exactly sure how to go about loving those who persecute me. Oh wait, that sounds like a Bible text. Ah yes, Matthew 5:44, 45: "I'm telling you to love your enemies. Let them bring out the best in you, not the worst. When someone gives you a hard time, respond with the energies of prayer, for then you are working out of your true selves, your God-created selves."

But how? Where is the "six-step plan" for loving creepy men whom I'm terribly afraid of? How am I supposed to show compassion to children who humiliate and mock me on the street?

Jesus never received justice on this earth either, so I realize that justice may be out of the question. And complaining gets me nowhere. But I am not God, and my humanity makes it difficult to learn how to love them.

After Bible study the leader approaches me and says she will pray that I do not leave Cambodia bitter. She is praying the same thing for herself. I suppose all of us are praying similar prayers.

"God help us to love those who seem unlovable, because, after all, we were unlovable first."

CHAPTER 40

$200

*"Never write about a place until you're away from it,
because that gives you perspective."*
—Ernest Hemingway

These days if I go for a walk it is after 5:00 p.m. when the heat and humidity are bearable, usually right before sunset. I leave the gated compound, walk past the guard, and brave the streets. I turn on my music, usually some acoustic folk music or Norah Jones. As I enter the eternally chaotic streets of Phnom Penh, I like to pretend the world around me is as peaceful as the soothing music I am listening to.

I have a 30-minute route that takes me down the least-congested roads. The road closest to home is a dirt one with potholes usually full of muddy water and food wrappers. At any time during the day, most Cambodians just sit outside and watch. So I serve as entertainment.

As I round the corner, I see a regular group of guys who play volleyball in an empty lot. Some play; others sit and watch. I've learned not to make eye contact with men. I've gotten really, really good at noting their presence but never acknowledging it. Some may be genuinely good and friendly people, yet I ignore them and keep walking.

I note the gathering of 25 or so men, speed up my steps, and keep my eyes forward. Over my music I hear them whistling and yelling something at me. It is not flattering. It is not welcome. And it is far from appealing. I keep walking.

As I pass an orphanage on the next corner, a young boy runs right at me. My heartbeat quickens, my eyes widen, and I gasp for breath. Feelings from the last time an innocent boy approached me rise instantly, and I eye him closely as he runs past me.

I cross the street of speeding motos and unfriendly stares. I've honestly started telling myself that people are just trying to decide if I am Nicole Kidman.

I think, *They'll realize I am not her and stop staring. Yup, any minute now. OK, they are still staring. They'll catch on soon.* It's the only way to feel less like a circus freak and more like a human being.

As I walk the road, my thoughts turn inward. This week Vitya was in a particularly good mood. Vitya is short and plump. He is the class clown and speaks, hands down, the best English. He almost always beats me to school even though I arrive an hour early. Usually he acknowledges me with a slight nod and pretends he has better things to be doing.

When the students walk into class each day, I stand at the door and greet them. Vitya has started standing in front of me and just waiting. I put out my hand to shake. He shakes his head no. I bow like the Japanese. He shakes his head no. I stand stiffly and salute. He looks disgusted as I attempt to greet him correctly.

Eventually, I jokingly give up and drop my chin to my chest. Then Vitya greets me in whatever way I hadn't thought of yet. Yesterday it was a high five. *Of course, why didn't I think of that?* This has turned into a ritual I look forward to each morning.

During break time he always makes his way to my desk and tells me whatever happens to be on his mind. This week it was politics.

"I hate Thai people, Vietnamese, and anyone else who has stolen land from Cambodia. Someday I build bomb, so they know who is boss."

He talks animatedly about the Khmer Rouge. He teaches me Khmer words I can use at the market. His laugh is a mischievous chuckle, and he produces a huge grin that automatically makes me laugh as well. Sometimes we arm wrestle. Sometimes I teach him Spanish words. Sometimes he tells me about the famous Ms. Hong, who was his American teacher last year and about how fabulous she was.

I secretly hope he annoys next year's student missionary about the famous Ms. Bo who was the greatest teacher ever! Most of the time Vitya talks and I just sit there and try to understand him.

I've realized that there really are three languages being spoken at school (in order of most common usage): Khmer, Khmer/English, and English. Students leave the last syllable sound off most words, add their whiny, nasal tone, and interject "uh," "um," "er," and "oy." Their English is a whole 'nother language.

One girl came up to me and said, "Cha Bo, di I paw the eggsa ah nawh?"

"What?" I asked.

Eventually, I worked out that she was saying, "Teacher Bo, did I pass the exam or not?"

Two Khmer workers look into our classroom. I am working at my desk. Vitya stomps up to me and jealously asserts, "I saw those guys. They were looking at you because you are so beautiful! Next time I see them I will hit them!"

I console him and promise him that I am OK, but I thank him for watching out for me. I smile as he returns to his desk.

I am brought back to reality as I dodge a little boy, maybe 2 years old, who is squatting in the middle of the street defecating. I shrug my shoulders and keep walking.

At the end of each day, households burn their rubbish in the street outside their homes. Coughing my way down one particularly smoky street, I pull my shirt over my nose and mouth and try not to think about the toxins filling my lungs while a little girl tosses more plastic bottles onto her fire.

I've decided I would pay $200 to be Cambodian for one day. What do they think when they look at me? I smile at women and children. They are safe. The women usually say "Sa-at," which means "beautiful." Do they wish they could give their children a better education? Do they wonder what I am doing here? Do they think I am like the American women they see in movies?

I round the corner to the mission where I live. Even weddings and funerals are held on the street, competing with honking horns, traffic, and yelling. A bright pink tent, tables and chairs, and an enormous speaker system have been set up. This event is a funeral because blasting through the speakers is a droning, repetitive recording of a Buddhist monk chanting religious beliefs. The sound can be heard for miles.

I walk through the gates, past the guard I cannot communicate with, and come home. Yes, I can call it home, and for now that doesn't feel strange at all.

CHAPTER 41

Audience

*"Close the door. Write with no one looking over your shoulder. Don't try to
figure out what other people want to hear from you; figure out what you have
to say. It's the one and only thing you have to offer."*
—*Barbara Kingsolver*

On this Friday morning at Cambodia Adventist School I find myself
speaking for chapel. I usually look forward to public speaking. It doesn't
bother me to get up in front of people; especially if I know what I'm saying
is important, as is the case today.

Looking over my audience of about a hundred high school students, I realize they are really listening to me. I had decided on a topic several weeks
ago after I heard a Khmer teacher speak at chapel. The last line of his talk
was as follows: "And remember, rape wouldn't happen if girls just put on
more clothes! Let's pray."

I was stunned. How could he say that? I couldn't stop thinking about his
message, so I decided to break the silence and respond to his presentation.

Because of the nature of the subject, my usual confidence is gone and my
voice quivers as I realize what I am about to say will either inspire them or
turn them away. I open my eyes from prayer. *This is it, I have to say something.*

"I've prayed a lot about whether to speak about this or not, and I feel like
I really need to. As you know, I am from the United States. I have been living
here for almost seven months, and I've learned a lot. I've also noticed a few
differences between Cambodia and the States."

I go on to mention the lighter side of my experiences: how crazy the traffic
is, the trash I hardly notice anymore, and the "lack of bubble" or personal
space that Cambodians have. They are all laughing really hard. They never
grow tired of these stories. They've been known to also keep laughing when
the conversation turns serious, but this time they don't.

"So there are many differences between Cambodia and the States. But I have to say, the hardest part about living in Cambodia is how some people react to me. Yes, I know, I am white. I am a foreigner, and I am reminded of it every day. I came to a foreign country, so, of course, people may stare. Women often smile and little children use their only-known English words: 'Hello! Hello!' But some Cambodian men have made me feel so low, unimportant, filthy, and worthless that I have, at many times, wanted to go home."

They are silent. They know I am serious. I read them my journal entry from the morning I was sexually assaulted back in January. I haven't really healed from this experience, and I know it when, in front of my students and several teachers, I am unable to read it without crying. But I finish the entry.

"I don't want to feel resentful toward the very people I came here to help." I go on to tell them about awful assaults that have happened to other foreign women I know. I can tell I am speaking new news to some of them and yesterday's news to others. Some of them peer back at me with mouths wide open, others with lips pursed shut. I am speaking to a split audience. Some of the students know this is going on but don't really care.

I am careful to ensure that they understand: not *all* Cambodian men are creeps. And coming to school each day reminds me that I know fabulous Cambodian citizens who would never do such things, and I thank them for it.

"So why am I telling you this? Well, I've decided that there is actually very little I can do, but so much you can do. I am powerless here, but you are powerful. This is your country. Are you OK with things the way they are? Do you like what people say about your country and what it stands for? I can't say I am proud of everything about the United States."

I talk about problems in the States. We have rapes, assaults, murder, robberies, prostitution, pornography, school shootings, alcoholism, drugs, and on and on. I want to make sure they understand I am not attacking their country.

"This world is broken. Do you care enough to fix it? I'm tired of hearing, 'Well, that's just the way it is in Cambodia!' Because what you are really saying is, 'Well, you should expect to get sexually assaulted. You are a foreigner, and that is how Cambodia treats foreigners.'

"No, it doesn't have to be this way. What are you going to do to change it? You don't have to be prime minister to do something. You just have to care enough to make a change, starting with yourself."

I tell them what the Great Commission says about going out and baptizing others, which doesn't mean the rest of us "nonpastors" are off the hook. It means we should take up the work closest to us and do what we know is right.

They are hearing me; I know they are. I have something important to say, and I am saying it. It is the closest to a "high" that I'll ever have, I suppose.

After closing prayer, an uncomfortable knot forms in my stomach when I realize that the less-mature students may be defensive and believe that I was just ranting against their country. If so, they missed the point.

Afterward I hide in my classroom. Chapel is the last period on Fridays, and they will all be going home soon. I don't want a bunch of awkward apologies because there's nothing else to say. I'm not seeking an apology from them. I realize this now.

They go home and I do too. But this time, upon entering the street on my bicycle and getting the same stares, comments, and kisses blown in my direction, they seem to have less power over me. The burden is a little lighter. I feel less alone and more understood. Not by the people along the way, but by students now making their way home, telling their parents about their day, and hopefully, thinking about what they just heard. More importantly, I hope they are thinking about how they, Cambodian citizens who feel virtually invisible, can do something to change the world.

This may all be absurdly high hopes for such a simple message. Changing the world isn't a revolutionary idea after all, but it is rarely mentioned in this corner of the globe. As for my meager attempts, these kids may be the only hope for this country. I'm just not sure they know it yet.

CHAPTER 42

The Faves

"Watch what God does, and then you do it, like children who learn proper
behavior from their parents. Mostly what God does is love you. Keep company
with him and learn a life of love. Observe how Christ loved us. His love was not
cautious but extravagant. He didn't love in order to get something from us but
to give everything of himself to us. Love like that."
—*Ephesians 5:1, 2*

Teachers who say they don't have their favorites are lying to you. I have favorites. Certain students make life easier nearly every day. I find strength to
come to school each day because these kids continue coming too.

Sayanet, an eleventh-grade girl, speaks freely and confidently. She hops
around and moves actively through the telling of her stories and jokes. She
will never claim beauty queen status because she says she doesn't care what
she looks like, but that's wonderful because she is incredibly beautiful without a speck of makeup. She's a tiny whiff of a person like all the girls here,
but her personality is so much more substantial. She rides her moto with a
helmet because she is smart, and accidents are common. She gets nearly
straight As because she is a hard worker. She wants to become a teacher and
help her country. Yeah, she is pretty great.

Leckanah, another delightful eleventh-grade girl with even more energy
and zest than Sayanet, makes class as lively as a late-night comedy club. Extremely petite, she is known as the class clown. She calls herself "Ms. World"
because one day she will be. She has an obsession with "chock-oh-late"—
you've got to hear her say it. She always wants to play games. She goes home
every day and watches TV, which is where she must get her jokes.

Surprisingly, I seem to relate best with the boys in my upper-grade classes.
Girls this age are usually silly, and the boys are stuck trying to figure them
out. I contribute what I can to their wonderings.

A few of the boys in tenth grade are hopeless romantics—Sokha, Sopheara, and Darithea. They practice singing love songs with a guitar between classes. They write about particular girls in their journals. They joke about who likes whom and giggle like fifth graders. I hope someday they will treat their wives right.

Another boy in my tenth-grade English class makes me smile every day. Ratanak usually waits near the door when I come in. He invites me to play soccer or volleyball with him and his friends. The other day they made a makeshift dartboard out of styrofoam and were throwing pens at it. I lost, but it is always nice to be asked to play. Even though Ratanak is a bit talkative in class, I have yet to get an evil glare from him when I ask him to be quiet. He looks at me when I talk to him, and he nods his head. Maybe he is listening.

I like Phalkun. She is the biggest Cambodian I have seen since I arrived here. She's far from overweight, but the people here are so tiny—she and I must look like giants compared to them.

Phalkun has chubby cheeks and dark eyes. She is such a tomboy. I've never seen her wear her hair down. She gives me high fives every time I walk past her. Sometimes she just sits and watches me type on the computer. The stares usually annoy me, but I'll miss hers when I leave.

Mariya is another girl who speaks excellent English. Also a tomboy, I seem to like those "real" kinds of girls. Oftentimes she will ask me a question about English I don't know the answer to. Instead of getting frustrated and rolling her eyes, she says, "You know what, Ms. Bo? There are a lot of things about Khmer I don't know either. It's OK. Don't worry about it!"

That is the most encouraging thing a student can say: "It's OK, you're human."

Mariya is tough. She puts a hat on as soon as the school bell rings. The other girls call her "fat" and "monkey." She just rolls her eyes and smiles halfheartedly. I wonder how much more she can let slide off her back.

Mariya approached me today and said, "Ms. Bo, I think now you a good teacher. Because when you have chapel talk about been attacked by Cambodian boy, you isn't make us feel bad like it is all Cambodians. You not biased because of one bad Khmer. You weren't look at us like you might see people on the street."

I could have cried. First, because of her compliment, and second, because I had taught her the word "biased" in English, and this was the first time she had used it correctly. Mariya was perceptive in noticing it may be difficult for me to teach Khmers. She said, in so many words, that she was glad I had noticed Cambodia is not a bad country, but that we just live in a bad world.

Daroth and Okhna are both smart, respectful, eighth-grade boys. They actually try in their schoolwork. They notice when I walk by instead of ignoring me or being immovable as I walk toward them. They are nice and respectful to girls. They don't roll their eyes at me or argue when I ask them to do something.

Daroth will make a great father some day. He is so good with little kids. Okhna is the "Beaver Cleaver" of Phnom Penh. He rides several miles to school each day on an old green bike, and he smiles the whole time. He doesn't notice the life-threatening traffic. Both of them actually study for geography tests and are easy to talk to. Sometimes, in the morning outside my classroom, I will hear this obnoxious but hilarious cackle of a laugh. I think Daroth is imitating something he saw on TV. I laugh every time.

An eighth-grade girl named Samdy also graces my classroom every day. This girl is special. She's curious about the world. She's always on time for school and laughs at my jokes, even when they aren't funny. She gives me flowers to put in my hair, and sometimes we sing *High School Musical* songs together.

She is responsible and efficient. She doesn't pretend to worship the ground I walk on just because I am white and a foreigner. She is friendly and a hard worker. She endures the heat of school for seven hours and then goes straight to work for a missionary family doing their laundry and watching their kids. She returns home after dark to a single mother. She does her homework, goes to bed, and lives the same reality day after day.

I could go on. While I do not look forward to the heat, the dirt, the construction workers drilling next door, or the eternally difficult students I face each day, I look forward to seeing Sayanet, Leckanah, Sokha, Sopheara, Darithea, Ratanak, Phalkun, Mariya, Daroth, Okhna, and Samdy. These kids are so great. I'm having a hard time finding the words.

These are the kids I'm raising money for. These are the students who deserve so much more than they are getting. They deserve futures and happiness and hope and success. These are the kids I am tearing up just writing about. Where did they come from, and why am I blessed to spend my days with them? How will I ever remember all they have taught me about suffering, relationships, their culture, and about truly living?

That's probably why I am still in Cambodia, and still writing.

CHAPTER 43

Pretending

"Yes, I am God. I've always been God and I always will be God. No one can take anything from me. I make; who can unmake it?"
—*Isaiah 43:13*

N ow remember, eighth grade, right after school today we will be having our runathon."

"Ahhhh, do we have to?" they groan. "We don't even have any sponsors and it's hot!"

Of course they don't have sponsors. Cambodians have never heard of a runa-whatever! They don't have money to spare anyway.

So they whine, "Why run around for half hour if we won't make no money?"

I don't want to tell them about the $3,000 that has already been raised back home. I still want them to work hard and not just depend on foreigners to hand them money. So I say, "Please, please just try. I'll run with you; we can race and see who can beat the teacher! It will be fun, and maybe we can get sponsors later. OK?"

They aren't convinced.

I spend the next two hours with the eleventh graders teaching English and morality. During English class they present oral book reports, which are usually pretty funny because of the way they put words together.

Today, Joanna says, "The house had big chicken where the family like be together."

After each report I usually correct a few errors, and after Joanna's I ask, "How did the family spend time together in a chicken?"

She looks at me blankly. "A chicken, Ms. Bo, where the family cooks?" She meant to say "kitchen" but instead said "chicken."

I'm glad that my classroom is a safe place to laugh and move on. We don't laugh to embarrass, but laughing at our mistakes makes it easier and more fun. Later I teach them the word "cocky" and kinda pop my collar in an overconfident, obnoxious sort of way. Granted, I am mimicking rap music artists whom I do not endorse, but almost everyone in my generation back home understands, so I teach my kids too.

Laughing later, I wonder, *What am I teaching these poor kids?* Now they are popping their collars at all the wrong times and circumstances. Oh, it is funny.

In tenth-grade English and speech/drama class, I teach them the song "I've Got the Feelin'." Today they all stop singing and doing the actions because I am so entertaining. I say and do things they would never imagine doing in public. Nothing scandalous, I promise! But things like speaking my opinion, making funny faces, and singing happily are not commonly done among the uber-shy Khmers.

Then, we pick roles for the upcoming Easter drama that will take place in April. Acting is as painful for them as having to skip rice at one single meal, which is absurd. Walking out the door, Chay Hak tosses me a volleyball. His English skills are coming along slowly, but we still understand each other. We bump the ball back and forth in the classroom, dodging fluorescent lights. We shake hands to agree that if one is broken we will split the cost. After one too many close calls, we stop, because neither of us really has money to pay for a new light anyway.

From here I go to teach the eighth-grade monkeys who call themselves students. They are playing soccer in the classroom with a plastic bottle. I dodge a goal kick as I walk through the door.

Some students, all girls, are studying for the geography quiz I have promised. Starting class, I realize that Vitya hasn't spoken to me in two weeks. I don't know why. He is a bit moody, which is unfortunate because he can be a lot of fun. It is hard enough feeling outnumbered by my students, but they also have a foreign language up their sleeve. Vitya is influential to the rest of the class, so I hope he gets over it soon.

At 3:00 p.m. the school bell rings and eight of my 24 students show up for the runathon. The students have innumerable reasons as to why they just can't stay for the fund-raiser. I tell them I am not going to force them to stay. So, in the oppressive Cambodian heat, the rest of us start running.

Fay and the principal help me count their laps and keep time. Sure, they take off sprinting at first with me bringing up the rear, but soon they are tired and walking. Cambodians love to play soccer, but they play on short corner streets and empty landfills. Many of them really aren't very fit and can't run long distances. After 30 minutes I have run 20 laps around the school's track, or about three miles. I am exhausted, dizzy, and have a headache. A few of the boys are right behind me and two brave girls pull up the rear. I am proud of them for trying.

Tomorrow I will tell the class that each student who ran in the runathon has a sponsor in the States who will pay for the laps they ran. Each student who ran will receive one dollar per lap. They earned it.

I come home and take the best shower I think I have ever experienced. Tim, Fay, and I watch a movie together in my room. It is now 8:40 p.m. and way past my bedtime—by one hour and 40 minutes.

I still live in Cambodia. I still ride my bike to school and try to be the teacher these kids need. I still feel distance from God. I am still fighting an eating disorder. Sometimes I feel depressed, and I cry and cry. I still miss home, and I may never fall in love with this country. But I'm still here and that's something.

Days like today are important. Today mattered to me. Today I realized that I fear loneliness because I have unconsciously believed that lonely people must be lonely because they are not loved. I know now that is not true.

As I think about all the people that love me and love these kids enough to sponsor them, I am reminded that I am not alone. There are people in the States who want me to succeed.

When I got up this morning, I decided that I was going to pretend that everything in my life was going smoothly. I pretended that I didn't have an eating disorder. I pretended that I felt like an adequate teacher. I pretended that I knew what God was doing with me here. I don't recommend pretending, but I recommend taking a humble moment to see what life would be like without the lies we tell ourselves.

As I pretended today, I felt peace, contentment, and absolute joy. Through living in a pretend world, I began to create new tapes to play to myself about what I want life to be like.

I'm learning that I don't have to be what I have been. It's terrifying, but it's good.

CHAPTER 44

Feminine

"Beauty is dangerous"
—*Gerard Manley Hopkins*

Beauty is dangerous and risky and scary and controversial and much more. I am obviously speaking from the female perspective, but hear me out.

I notice a significant difference in the attitude of my students if I wear a new skirt or wear my hair down. It's a big deal. The boys are more quiet and shy, and they look me up and down. The girls are more worshipful and giggly. It is kind of ridiculous that they make such a big deal about what I look like, as if that is my primary focus in life. They will talk on and on about how beautiful my hair is or how stylish my clothes are.

If being the most beautiful person in the world was my only goal in life, then I would be flattered. But living in a country where white skin is favored and adored no matter what you look like, it doesn't feel so special anymore. I thought I was escaping shallowness by leaving the States, but I guess I was wrong.

Beauty is especially dangerous on the street. My usual uniform for town is a white T-shirt, boy-cut khaki shorts, and Crocs. Many times, I pull my hair back like an uptight librarian or just wear a hat. I wear my SARS mask and big sunglasses. If I'm riding a moto, I wear a helmet, not merely to be safe but to hide.

That is what I do wear, but there are things I won't wear. I wouldn't dare wear high heels for fear it would attract more attention. Hey, I don't even *own* high heels! Nail polish is not an option, and I haven't used a blow-dryer or curling iron since I've been here. I never show my shoulders, much of my legs, or anything low cut. Granted, it is good to dress modest no matter what country you live in, but I live in Cambodia where I fear looking like a woman because of the curses, the stares, and the touching.

I fear looking like a woman because in many people's eyes I am "just asking for it." I don't think dressing like a woman has to mean showing a lot of skin, dressing provocatively, or wearing layers of makeup. I would just like to wear a flowing skirt, something pretty, or wear my hair down. But I usually don't. Too risky. This is no time for beauty. I don't feel feminine here. But why would I want to? The only thing that femininity gets me is being treated like a prostitute.

I've thought a lot about how this relates to my eating disorder. After I was attacked in January I binged more than usual because I didn't want to be attractive enough to be touched that way ever again.

My counselor told me that she substituted for an alcoholics' group session one time. She said you wouldn't be able to tell the difference between our eating disorder group sessions and the alcoholics' session. Same issues, same conversations, just a different weapon.

At one point one of the members turned to her and said, "We know you aren't an alcoholics' counselor. Why do you think you can understand us?"

"Well," she responded, "the core issues of control and self-hatred and escape are the same, with one major difference. Alcoholics need to wean themselves away and eventually go cold turkey from their addiction. Those with eating disorders must indulge in their addiction several times a day and *still* get better. That is like forcing an alcoholic to become sober while entering a bar three times a day and drinking."

My counselor is optimistic that people can fully recover from eating disorders. I'm not so sure anymore. Unfortunately, there is more supporting evidence for the opposite idea that people never recover.

My ED has definitely gotten worse since I have been here. I will at least agree that being here has made me stronger, but I wonder if being stronger has also turned me into steel. I wonder if being stronger has made me insensitive. I wonder if being stronger has made me cynical.

I wonder a lot of things I just can't answer right now. Mostly I feel attacked on all sides with no chance of relief until I get home. Ten months is a long time to keep fighting.

A lifetime is way longer.

CHAPTER 45

Cultured Out

*"Unlike the culture around you, always dragging you down
to its level of immaturity, God brings the best out of you,
develops well-formed maturity in you."*
—Romans 12:2

I made it to Australia. At present, I am proud of myself for booking my tickets, applying for a visa, figuring out travel details, converting my money, using an AU pay phone, buying train tickets, and riding the train to Gosford where I meet up with my friends. I did it all without my mom. Amazing.

It is shocking to suddenly be surrounded by people who look like me and talk like me. There are so many blond heads and blue eyes.

In Gosford, Australia, I meet up with Ross and Kamrong. We are all here for vacation during the Khmer New Year celebrations in Cambodia. He is Australian and she is Khmer, so that's how they ended up traveling between the two countries. We go in search of kangaroos and feed them the only food in the car: cornflakes. We drive to Avondale Adventist College, where I meet up with Bryce, a friend from high school.

After church on Sabbath, Bryce shows me the campus, and then we head to the beach with some of his friends. Later that week he takes me to an Australian football game. It is a cross between rugby, soccer, football, basketball, and a wedding. My favorite part is when the player tosses the ball over his shoulder like a bouquet and whoever gets it has the next possession. Laughter, jokes, pointless fun, and late nights mark my visit and remind me of the college life I've been missing.

I eat in a McDonald's. The streets are spotless. People use trash cans, and I am completely ignored on the street. I am understood by the people I talk to. It feels good to laugh. I've missed feeling funny. Feeling understood is something I'll never again take for granted.

I call my parents and two of my best friends in Nebraska, Rachael and Katelyn. I try to explain to them the difference between Australia and Cambodia, but I'm not sure I can. The most common thought running through my head is, *How is it possible that Cambodia and Australia exist simultaneously? They are so extremely different. I just don't understand.*

After visiting Gosford we travel to Sydney. The Sydney Opera House is beautiful. Although it is raining, I take the train to the City Centre and walk around in the cold. I can't tell exactly how cold it is but compared to the 95-degree weather I am accustomed to, it feels like I'm freezing.

I stroll to the opera house and take some pictures. It is inspiring to see beautiful, creative masterpieces at the Museum of Contemporary Art. I visit the botanical gardens and watch street performers. What a nice day.

I spotted a bookstore yesterday that I fully intend inhabiting for several hours today. I know, I know, I am in Australia, and instead of seeing the sights I'm languishing in a bookstore?

Yeah, you would too if you had been deprived for months. If I was coming here from the States with friends, my itinerary would be different. But since I'm coming alone from Cambodia, all I want to do is sit and watch people walk by. I want to soak up the clean streets and the manicured lawns. I want to take pictures of flowers I have seen hundreds of times back home. I want to sit on the train and listen to people speak English. Strangely, all I want to eat is Asian food, but that is another story.

Places like Australia do exist! The whole world hasn't turned into Cambodia. I don't have to live like this forever.

I love the fact that people ignore me here and that I feel skinny again. I've been living in a country where the average girl is a size zero.

So have I learned anything? Can I live a more comfortable life but remember that not everyone does? Do I have to live in squalor the rest of my life to understand poverty, to truly help and understand those less fortunate? Can we achieve balance, or do we merely say that as we sit in our wonderful homes and experience fine education? Will I feel guilty the rest of my life? Tomorrow I plan to see the Art Gallery of New South Wales, which has free admission and free aboriginal dances at noon. I've already visited all of the free sights in town: the opera house, the Sydney Observatory, and the botanical gardens. With the income of a student missionary this free route is basically my only option.

My time in Australia is quickly coming to an end. Monday morning will find me right back in 95-degree temperatures, teaching and living in a culture I don't understand. I need everyone's prayers because I feel a bit cultured out. From the U.S. to Cambodia, Cambodia to Thailand, Thailand to Cambodia, Cambodia to Malaysia, Malaysia to Cambodia, Cambodia to Australia, and then back again, I don't think I fit in anywhere.

All of these culture shifts have left me seeking to control my life in any way possible. Unfortunately, that control seems to be manifested in binging and purging. Many evenings this week I've found myself kneeling over a toilet trying to avoid problems that will never be solved that way.

Today I sit at the train station, alone, and watch a woman return home from her commute. She approaches a warm waiting car, which I assume is driven by her husband. I watch as they kiss and no doubt head home. I want a home.

CHAPTER 46

Starbucks and Escalades

"One day a traveler dropped in on the rich man. He was too stingy to take an animal from his own herds or flocks to make a meal for his visitor, so he took the poor man's lamb and prepared a meal to set before his guest."
—2 Samuel 12:4

What did you do for your vacation from school?"

My eighth graders are especially chatty after not seeing their friends for over a week.

"Vanny got a girlfriend," someone quips from the back row.

"Sombhat was out partying," says another.

The bantering about everyone *else's* vacation continues.

"OK, OK. Well, I went to Australia and it was great," I say.

Since Vitya has stopped shunning me, he comes up and says, "You go Aust-trail-lea and what you bring me?"

I pretend to look a bit flustered and respond, "A big hug?"

He grins and continues, "You leave Thursday, what you do? I want whole thing. Day-by-day." Vitya then bends over, puts his elbows on my desk, his chin in his hands, and flutters his eyelashes. He looks genuinely interested.

"Well, um, I saw the beach and some kangaroos. It was really cold."

But he stops me several times and says, "You skip something? I want all. Don't skip. Now go back, say that part again."

In drama class we practice our play for this weekend's Easter program. It isn't Easter, but Cambodians don't really celebrate it anyway, so it doesn't matter what weekend we celebrate it.

I picked Chamrong to be Jesus because I knew Chamrong would complain the least. Is it wrong to punish the good kids because I know they won't complain? Probably so, but I did it anyway.

We are practicing a scene where Jesus, or Chamrong, is healing people who come to him. So Somphos is pretending to have a broken leg. Apparently, Chamrong likes Somphos, so the action of "healing" her by touching her leg makes the whole class swoon and giggle uncontrollably. Oh, the immaturity of teenagers.

My next class is eleventh-grade morality class where they ask if I brought them a kangaroo.

"Well, I tried." My Australian accent kicks in. "But I was sneaking through the brush and the kangaroo saw me coming. I ran swiftly through the grass as fast as my legs would carry me. I finally snuck up on him and wrapped my arms around his neck. He was fighting and kicking and saying, 'Please, no, no, don't take me!'"

The eleventh graders laugh wildly at my act, so I continue.

"I wrestled the kangaroo to the ground and pulled out my suitcase to put him in, but he refused to fit inside. I guess he just didn't understand how badly you wanted to see a kangaroo. Isn't that rude?"

Navy looks completely convinced by my story until the others tell her I'm joking.

The construction crew is drilling today, as they do every other day. They are drilling and pounding about 12 feet from my classroom. I am trying to teach double negatives to no avail. They just can't hear me.

I yell, "So, when you are speaking, don't use double negatives such as 'don't not.'"

Sixty eyeballs look at me like I am crazy. I give up. Not today. We all start laughing as I drop my shoulders, let out a deep sigh, and close my textbook. I start writing things on the board because that is the only way to be "heard."

After class Rithea comes up to me and proudly says, "Ms. Bo, you know I can dunk basketball?"

"Oh really? I didn't think Cambodians played basketball."

I highly doubt that he can dunk, but I listen politely and smile. Once I am around the corner and out of view, I laugh. It feels good to laugh. I thought today would be rough. But it was OK. No, it was fun.

Last week I walked the streets of Sydney, completely in awe of my surroundings. Now I am back in Cambodia, which is about 20 years behind the rest of the developed world—about the life span of the Khmer Rouge. (It obviously didn't help to eradicate all the highly educated people in the country.) Yes, we have computers that hum and occasional Escalades that cruise the streets here. But as a culture, maturity and technology are way behind.

As I sweat in the heat and chaos of Cambodia, the busy trains of Sydney continue to run. As I watch a new mother hold her naked child, Starbucks serves up another cup of coffee. As I dish out my 50 cents for lunch today, a shopper in Coach purchases a $4,000 bag.

No, it doesn't make sense.

Twenty percent of the world lives on less than a dollar a day. That makes me want to secretly dive in to the other 80 percent's bank accounts and withdraw just a dollar or 10 to even things out. I am convinced that that is all it would take. If everyone was actually aware of these inequities, they would do something about it. Right?

Instead, just as I have done and fear doing upon returning home, we create comfortable environments to distract ourselves from the fact that the world and its inhabitants are hurting. I suppose I'm just freshly overwhelmed at how to solve the problem that people have been trying to solve for centuries. It seems so hopeless.

But today I laughed in Cambodia. I am still frustrated by the world's situation and by the people I deal with every day. But part of me felt proud to be helping, at least right now, in a small way. I did what I could amidst the heat, construction, and confusion. I laughed because, well, it was all I could do. At least for today.

CHAPTER 47

All Is Well

"Understanding is curing ignorance and curing ignorance is abolishing fear."
—Matt Marty

Today I get out my box of letters and notes I have received since arriving in Cambodia. The box is full. I just kept slipping in the cards as they came. I had no idea how many were in there. A lot. I read each one over again: cards from my mom and my sister, letters and drawings that my friends have sent my way, "I'm praying for you" reminders from Union students and teachers.

Even my 6-year-old cousin Oriel sent me notes and drawings, one saying, "you or my sunshin My onle SUNSHIN you mak me hAPe wiN skis or GRAy you wiL NEVR no der HAW much I Love you pLes dot. tak my sunshin uway." (Why don't we spell words as they really sound? She is a smart girl.)

Leaving the U.S. has helped me see my faults more clearly. America is just another country on the globe. On a spiritual level, we need as much help as any country I have visited. I have met people from all over the world: Thailand, Malaysia, Australia, Cambodia, Vietnam, Sri Lanka, Pakistan, India, England, Laos, and Burma. Some of these countries have started sending missionaries to the States. Why?

"Americans are the hardest to witness to," they tell me. "You think you know everything. You think you have heard it all. You are the unreachable."

They say we think we don't need saving.

I have learned a lot in Cambodia. I understand a little better. Not fully. Better.

I have a better understanding of what a rape victim feels like when after being assaulted she is ashamed to tell someone. That never made sense to me until after the morning I was attacked; I considered never telling anyone. I thought that maybe, in some sick way, it was my fault.

I have a better understanding of why women end up with abusive men. They want to feel love somewhere or even once in a while instead of never.

I have a better understanding of why people use drugs. We all have our own weapons of self-destruction and drugs seem awfully appealing when the pain seems too much to bear.

I have a better understanding of why people become alcoholics. I have wanted to be numb to life sometimes too. Some days the poverty on the street is just too much. How many times can someone wake up to the same miserable existence, unable to quiet their hungry children?

I have a better understanding of the children that curse at me. The story of their short lives thus far would cause most people to cry. They've become tough in order to cope.

I'm beginning to better understand why Khmers are always late, why they have such extreme loyalty to their families, and why they don't seem to get road rage when infinite opportunities exist!

I am no genius. I don't have this all figured out. I feel guilty wanting to come home when my kids here will never experience the comforts that I do.

I saw a magazine ad this week that made me want to scream. It was a picture of a beautiful man and woman sitting on the deck of a beautiful home on a beautiful lake. The ad was for some deck company and the copy read: "A '99 Pinot. Bare feet. A sunset. All is well in the universe."

I wanted to rip it out and tear it up and scream and yell. I wanted to say, "NO! All is *not* well with the universe! Have you ever heard of AIDS? Have you seen the homeless people in our cities? Have you ever witnessed bleeding, unending injustice?"

We have. But we try to pretend we haven't.

I'm scared to fall back into that mentality once I leave: the idea that just because I am OK, the rest of the world must be too.

CHAPTER 48

Now and Then

"We do not grow absolutely, chronologically.
We grow sometimes in one dimension, and not in another; unevenly.
We grow partially. We are relative. We are mature in one realm, childish
in another. The past, present, and future mingle and pull us backward,
forward, or fix us in the present.
We are made up of layers, cells, constellations."
—Anais Nin

Meeting Polly Yoder is the third-best thing to happen to me since I arrived in August. The number one best thing is having Tim and Fay Scott here. Number two was moving in with Tim and Fay back in January.

Polly and I met at the end of February, and she has been a blessing to me ever since. For example she stopped by a few minutes ago on her way home from school just to see how my day was! She is like the kinds of friends I have back home and have missed dearly since I've been here. She is an incredible answer to prayer.

She comforts me, she challenges me to think, and she prays for me and means it. She invites me over to do absolutely nothing, knowing how much I just need company. She listens, she is honest, and she is funny.

We are going to Vietnam together in two weeks with another friend of ours, Megan. She has introduced me to a whole community of great people from Logos Christian School, where she teaches. The principal's wife invited me out for coffee the other night. Marie, another Bible study friend, offered the help of a counselor friend of hers. One of Polly's roommates offered me her English lesson plans to help with my classes. Polly invited me to attend her church, International Christian Fellowship.

This is community. This is having more than one person to talk to. This is comforting. This is what I have needed for so long. This is the closest thing

I am going to get to home. This is what will carry me through.

This afternoon I sit, watching 13 seniors from Logos Christian School wave goodbye to their childhood and step into the future. They are graduating. Polly invited me along and the experience is bringing up my own high school memories.

Savoring every moment—the optimism, excitement, and energy—I remember looking that way. I honestly thought I had everything figured out my senior year in high school at 18 years old. I remember feeling that way. Has it been only two years since that moment?

At that point I was already struggling with an eating disorder I didn't understand; of course, I still don't fully understand it. I was not about to admit I had a problem because I honestly didn't think I did. Everyone just kept complimenting me on how great I looked, and the compliments kept coming the longer I starved myself. I didn't know who I was, but apparently I was pretty, headed to college, and life was good.

That seems so long ago. Now, I look beat-up, calloused, and weary. What I thought the future held for me after high school has been lost somewhere. I guess my expectations weren't incredibly specific, I just never thought I'd be here. Not necessarily *here*, in Cambodia. But here, tired, confused, frustrated, lost, and feeling homeless.

Not that I want high school back. I was more than happy to exit that chapter of my life. But a lot has changed, and I don't know who Heather is anymore. This worries me.

All of this pondering reminded me of a sermon I heard about worries, so I make a list of 10 of my current worries:

1. finding a roommate for next school year
2. getting a job next year
3. readjusting to American life and forgetting everything that I've learned
4. what I've turned into
5. never finding God, or worse, living the rest of my life pretending I have
6. bulimia sticking with me the rest of my life
7. binging and purging tonight and this weekend
8. leaving Cambodia bitter and angry
9. always letting people down
10. home not being the heaven I expect it to be

None of these worries existed the day I graduated from high school. And today, I can't do a single thing about anything on that list, which is annoying. Apparently, it holds true, "This is a journey. Let life happen." This is my daily mantra.

CHAPTER 49

God Fast

"I know God will not give me anything I can't handle.
I just wish He didn't trust me so much."
—Mother Teresa

Stella is a short Indian woman. She has a wonderful accent and a nose ring. She is 49 years old. She wears bright silk garments that make me wish it would somehow be normal for me to come back from Cambodia and start dressing like an Indian. Stella is warm and her voice is calming. Stella is my counselor.

I used to have a counselor back home. But we lost contact. Through meeting Polly and the Logos group, many good things have come into my life, including Stella. I ride my bike to her house once a week and we just talk. I've needed another friend.

After returning from Australia and telling my Bible study group about my eating disorder, they recommended I see Stella. I might not have consented because I'm close enough to going home. But I need help; I've needed help all year. I'm glad to have found her. I've learned a lot from this woman. I want to believe what she says. I want to live how she does.

She tells me it's OK to feel anger toward the men who continue to torment me on the street. She tells me that my experience in Cambodia has been far from normal. She says I'm very brave. She tells me that having an eating disorder is not a sin. The last one is hardest to believe.

I tell her my frustrations with constantly striving to see and understand a God whom I just do not see or understand.

"Heather, why don't you give this god stuff a break? If God is God, isn't He big enough and caring enough to find you? If you admit you are sick and tired of trying so hard and coming up with nothing, don't you think He'll see that?" she concludes.

Although Stella is a Christian, the idea sounds sacrilegious and atheistic. "Won't giving up the search just take me further away from ever finding God?"

"Darling, I think God wants you to rest in Him, not fight day in and day out to experience Him."

So, oxymoronic as it may sound, I'm fasting from God. I'm not stressing about my relationship with Him or what I am doing or not doing. If it happens naturally, like singing a praise song or offering up a quick prayer, I'm not avoiding it, but otherwise, I'm not beating myself up for all the spiritual things I'm not doing.

I haven't binged or purged in almost a week. Stella has been helping with that too. Every night after dinner I call her to tell her what I ate. Accountability is good. I feel better, yet lost at the same time. This is definitely a journey. I can see the end of my time in Cambodia, and I think that helps.

I looked at pictures on my laptop this week: pictures from my senior class trip, graduation, and Union College, basically the last three years of my life. Looking at the past, I realize that I used to play basketball and wasn't too bad. I used to enjoy playing the piano. I am pretty sure I used to enjoy cooking. I used to scrapbook. I used to have quite a few friends around me. I used to sit at Barnes and Noble for hours and be completely content.

This may sound ridiculous, but when I got here nine months ago, nobody really cared about my past or where I came from. Anything before August 22, 2007, no longer mattered, so I started from scratch.

Some of my favorite hobbies, habits, and tendencies could no longer exist in my new environment. And obviously the people I used to be surrounded by weren't here either. I've been absorbing, learning, and changing since my plane landed, which makes me anxious about home. I don't recognize the wrinkly, defeated-looking girl in the mirror. I look tired. I am tired. I'm basically just waiting to exhale.

Taking a break from reflecting on my past, I watch *The Killing Fields*, a film about the recent war in Cambodia. I haven't seen it before, and watching this movie in Cambodia is quite an experience. It is interesting to see what Phnom Penh looked like several years ago and to somewhat comprehend the language they use in the movie. It also reminds me of the remnants of war that still exist in this country, if you know what you are looking for.

Liver cancer is a huge problem among Khmer Rouge survivors because of the starvation they endured.

The mind-your-own-business and toughen-up attitude comes directly from the years where dog-eat-dog survival was required and still is. Some people don't stop when they hit foreigners riding bicycles or care where the trash gets put because it is not their problem. Cheating is encouraged in some families. Success and making money are so crucial; they don't really care how they acquire it. Some Khmers can't be trusted and in turn do not trust others. Why would they? They've seen how quickly evil can manifest into genocide.

There are still Khmer Rouge officers living in the humongous mansions that dot this city. Some officers are tried in court and sent to jail. Others pay the court system enough money to avoid the penalties they deserve.

Land mines continue to detonate in the countryside. Some explode from NGO de-mining groups; others explode on farmers.

Watching *The Killing Fields* reminds me that I am still living in an extremely broken, war-torn country. The fighting ended only eight years ago. According to my Khmer friends, the movie is fairly accurate, yet cut short. What the movie shows was only the beginning of a horrific 25-year war.

I'm reminded of why I'm here. I'm not sure how I have survived the last nine months, but I'm still here. The time has definitely not whizzed by like other SMs said it would, but I've almost made it.

CHAPTER 50

Adequate and More

"Our deepest fear is not that we are inadequate.
Our deepest fear is that we are powerful beyond measure.
It is our light, not our darkness that most frightens us.
We ask ourselves, Who am I to be brilliant, gorgeous, talented, fabulous?
Actually, who are you not to be? You are a child of God.
Your playing small does not serve the world.
There is nothing enlightened about shrinking
so that other people won't feel insecure around you.
We are all meant to shine, as children do.
We were born to make manifest the glory of God that is within us.
It's not just in some of us; it's in everyone.
And as we let our own light shine,
we unconsciously give other people permission to do the same.
As we are liberated from our own fear, our presence
automatically liberates others."
—*Marianne Williamson*

I've decided I'm a good teacher.

I'm a good teacher because I'm fun. I teach English grammar every day, and we have fun doing it. I'll admit I don't always have the most creative ideas for teaching noun clauses, but I do what I can. I sing parts of the lesson, I find ways to incorporate dancing or wiggling for much-needed emphasis, and I make up funny examples to keep them interested. I smile a lot. I laugh a lot. They are still popping their collars and making me laugh in return.

In speech class last week, I tried to imitate my college teacher Mr. Blake's method. As the first student finished his speech, I started cheering and clapping and hollering and doing my best to show him he was awesome. They all looked at me, obviously surprised, and laughed.

"Yahoo!" I squealed excitedly, "Ya-hoo!"

All the students turned around to better view the spectacle sitting behind them. Smiles spread as one ornery student, David, yelled, "Gmail!"

Now, catching on, he and the other students kept clapping and cheering randomly, "Hotmail! AOL!"

They were really just mocking me, but it was still side-splitting fun!

I'm a good teacher because I'm tough. In high school I never got away with laziness, why should they? Oh, they argue that none of their other teachers expect as much as I do, but I expect papers to be in on time, and I take off points if they aren't. Sure, I offer the occasional "gracification," but I have high expectations, and they are rising to meet them. I expect work to be done well and without cheating. My classroom is quiet, and when it isn't, I am just as annoying as my teachers were. I pause, look at them, and say, "Oh, I'll wait till you're done talking. Are you finished?"

I'm a good teacher because I'm easygoing. Sometimes my kids are just having one of those days and there is nothing penetrating except the seemingly huge problem on their mind. I encourage them to meet me after school so that we can work on it together. If the kids are honest about their struggle to complete something they don't understand, I do my best to help them. I make deals with students who I know are hard workers. If they don't slack off at school, yet had one rough weekend, I give them the break they need.

I'm a good teacher because I care. I do not humiliate my kids. I don't criticize them in class or announce grades up front. I do my best to be fair and kind, and even though I often want to give F's to the obnoxious boys, I don't.

I'm a good teacher because I'm learning every day how to read each of them a little better. Youran can't look me in the eyes, so I kneel next to him when I talk, and I always end up whispering like he does. Most students fear Vandeth, including me sometimes, because of his arrogance. So, I do my best to ease the tension he creates in class every day. One student described him as "destructive." Somphos is painfully shy about the kids teasing her about an apparent romance with Chamrong. So, when the tenth graders start ranting and raving, I change the subject and start joking about everyone else's love lives. It always works. Vitya likes to ask painfully obvious questions when he is lonely. He just wants to start conversations with me in any way possible. I flatter him and try to be patient even when I am late for class or dead tired.

I'm a good teacher because I'm honest. I don't unload on my kids or anything, but I tell them what they need to know. I tell them what I need from them and encourage them to be equally honest. I think this is how Sayanet and I have become pretty close. After a few rough patches of gaining her confidence, we just seem to "get" each other now.

Today is a rough day for Sayanet. She has tears in her eyes the whole time I teach and keeps her head down on her desk. She won't talk to anyone. I talk to her after school. "Sayanet, I'm so proud of you for letting other people see your pain today. If you are mad, be mad. If you are overwhelmed, be overwhelmed. Just don't hold it all in until it explodes. Let people see that you feel. You will get help if you ask for it."

"Well, if I do that I will make people around me sad." This is a common belief. They pretend their way through life so they aren't a burden on anyone, including close friends and family members.

"I can't speak for everyone you know, but your sadness doesn't force me to be miserable," I assure her. "When you show your emotions it helps me understand you better, and then I can help you. I want to know all of you, not just the happy side. No one is perfect. We all have bad days, and I want to hear about them."

This is the part of teaching I *love*: really connecting with a student one-on-one, knowing she's getting it. She is quiet and stares at the ground as she soaks it all in.

After a long while, she says "thank you" several times before leaving, which is a very un-Khmer thing to do.

I realize that I cannot have experiences like this every day, but I'm a good teacher because I try to connect on a deeper level with my students.

I'm not sure if teaching is my life calling, but I'm learning to enjoy this experience. First of all, this isn't real teaching. Well, not *real* by American standards. So granted, I'm not really a teacher yet, I'm a volunteer posing as a teacher.

Secondly, I hate, *hate* grading papers, writing lesson plans, and calculating final scores. I just want to spend time with these kids. They've taught me several of their strange jokes and fun games. They've taught me patience; oh, how they've taught me patience. They've taught me that helping others is fabulous medicine for a selfish soul. They've taught me that I don't know the first thing about what it means to have a "hard" life. They've taught me that I can always be more flexible. They've taught me that maybe I can slow down a bit, maybe I can just sit and be with them instead of talking so much.

I didn't know what I wanted to do with the rest of my life, so I came to Cambodia to take a break and figure things out. I still don't know what I want to do with the rest of my life, but it turns out Cambodia had a few things to teach me that Nebraska never could.

I'm taking these lessons and holding on to them for dear life.

CHAPTER 51

Rays of Hope

*"If you lose hope, somehow you lose the vitality that keeps life moving,
you lose that courage to be, that quality that helps you go on in spite of it
all. And so today I still have a dream."*
—*Martin Luther King, Jr.*

A good friend wrote me an e-mail saying, "Heather, if life were an orange, you squeeze out more juice than anyone I know!" I think that is a compliment. I'm choosing to take it as a compliment. Either way, it made me laugh out loud at the Internet shop down the street.

I've been thinking a lot about this year: the good and the ugly. I have noticed that humans in general and myself specifically tend to dwell on the bad instead of the good. For example, my time in Cambodia sounds as if it has been an eternal dark, grey cloud. With the help of depression and a mental illness or two, it has seemed that way. But I know better.

Rays of hope have kept me here. Unfortunately, I shove these rays of hope to the back of my mind whenever something else is thrown at me.

Negativity is a defense against hard times. I have started expecting difficulties, so they are easier to deal with. If I brace myself for the tormentors waiting on the street, they are easier to bear. But often I brace myself expecting difficulties, and they never come. Still, instead of rejoicing or being grateful, I just hold my breath, expecting a harder blow next time.

When I first arrived, the Scotts welcomed me with open arms, and they have continued to support me better than anyone here. They've been a listening ear, a source of wisdom, a help, and a comfort; they are wonderful friends. I have had a great place to live: clean, safe, nourishing; a refuge from the storms outside and the storms inside.

During these months I have met some incredible teachers at CAS. JC, for example, saw that I needed help and friendship. He helped with my loneliness by taking me out on the weekends, and in turn, I was adopted by his friends from Mission College where they all graduated. I had somewhere to go on weekends when I was truly lonely, and that meant so much. We don't always understand each other; our cultures are so different, but we have learned.

I've found another ray of hope in my students. For the first four months, teaching was torture. I had no idea what I was doing or where to start. At first my students were the enemy; now, they are friends. These kids helped me along, forgave me when I didn't know the answers to all their questions, and taught me how to teach. Their humor and easygoing attitude made class less scary and something to look forward to. When I was experiencing awful days and home was the only thing on my mind, I was forced to put that aside, walk into the classroom, and be present with them. They eased the homesickness by producing the laughter and the smiles I needed.

I have had the privilege—no, honor—of meeting and learning from people from all over the world. I have listened intently to their stories, hoping to gain just an ounce of their wisdom that far exceeds my own. Stories of flying bricks, fires, anti-Christian movements, and true persecution will always stay with me. They've taught me what commitment really looks like.

I have been blessed with even more. The fact that I can use Skype to simultaneously talk to my parents in Colorado, my sister and Ben in Nebraska, and my brother in England, still amazes me every time. I have been able to receive encouragement and strength via e-mail from people I never expected would notice I was gone.

I have received letters, postcards, and more packages than any other SM Fay has ever seen. Loved ones helped me raise more than $8,000 for Cambodia Adventist School and the Vietnamese school where I tutored. That's a huge amount of money! I am proud of my supportive friends and family back home.

I am grateful for so many other things. Slowly, I'm trying to look at life in a more positive way. I'm thankful that I have not contracted any vicious disease—bird flu didn't get me.

I could've been injured badly when I was hit by that car, but I wasn't.

I could've been physically harmed just about any time I took to the streets, but I haven't been badly injured.

I could've never met Polly. I could've never met Stella.

I could be poor. I could be an orphan.

I could be so many things, but I am not.

So, for whatever it's worth, this is where I am at right now. I know at least two of my friends who are headed out to be student missionaries next year. Part of me wants to say, "Don't do it! It's gonna hurt." But the human soul buried deep down inside of me says, "Go."

CHAPTER 52

Voice of a Canary

*"I'm so grateful to Christ Jesus for making me adequate to do this
work. He went out on a limb, you know, in trusting me with this ministry.
The only credentials I brought to it were invective and witch hunts and
arrogance. But I was treated mercifully because I didn't know what I
was doing—didn't know Who I was doing it against!"*
—1 Timothy 1:12, 13

I have two weeks and three days left in Cambodia. Things are wrapping up.
I'm taking a lot of pictures and reflecting even more than usual.

Today, I wake up and am glad it is Friday. I've been having a lot of dreams
the last few weeks.

My dreams have been exhausting and find me failing to adjust at home or
getting raped in Cambodia. I often wake up in tears. Walking out the door
to face another day in Cambodia after such crazy dreams is difficult.

I am done teaching new lessons, so reviewing has started for final tests.
My kids understand that I'm leaving soon. For my students' last journal entry,
I asked them to write me a letter. I wasn't specific as to what it had to say.
This was one of the first times they didn't complain about the assignment.
I've needed these words:

"Since I studied in the CAS I have met three foreign teachers. Some
were so strict I felt scared of them, but you were a teacher that work and
laugh with the students. Sometimes, you also danced and sang for the students."—Heang

"It was very hard to getting to know you, because I didn't know you before, and in the first two months I also hated you so much. But many times
passed away, I felt that my thought has been changed. Many times that I tired
or bored, you encouraged my mind and I felt that you liked me and you
gave the warmth to me anytime I needed."—Phalkun

"All the times you sang, I felt sleepy but it not mean that your voice is horrible but because your voice is soft like a canary."—Rachana

"You are a good teacher and you are so friendly. Sometimes act like a kid and sometimes like an old person. All of these words is from my heart, and it is not mean that I want to get more points from you."—Samdy

"In the time for studying you always have teached student by friendly and happy everytime. Even though, that student always disturbed, speaking with each other, and talked a bad word to you. You never angry to they, you always smile and talk to them by soft word."—Angelina

"Last year my class was a big problem or virus for school. We made a lot of troubles, but this year, we all were changing because of you. You are changing us. Now I know that you by which the environments around me have changing me and all of us. I never have a good teacher as you since I studied here. You're my best teacher ever and ever."—Ratanak

"Ms. Bo, to be honest, I didn't like you very much at the beginning of the year. But day by day, I realized that are a great teacher and I started to like you. Ms. Bo, you might think that you are not a great teacher, but that isn't true. I enjoyed every moment you spent with us. I just want to let you know that words alone cannot express how great you are to be our teacher and how much we love you. God bless you and your whole family. May He also protect you on the way back home."—David

I have read and reread the words of my students. If I had this encouragement all year, it might have been a little easier. But, as noted, they didn't feel this way about me all year! From their perception though, I've done OK.

I thought back to my years of high school. In high school I committed to writing letters to the teachers who had honestly changed me in meaningful ways. One of my teachers approached me in tears, thanking me for the encouragement. Now I understand why: because we all need it so much. Why are we so stubborn and reluctant to let people know how great they are?

It is not possible to encourage someone too much. So, on that note:

Thank you, Mrs. Simpson. You taught me that I did not have to fall in love with math; I just had to pass. At 6:45 a.m. most weekday mornings, you offered help with Algebra II and help with life.

Thank you, Mr. Williams, for your patience, your kind heart, and your sense of adventure in a chemistry class you've taught over and over again for more than 20 years.

Thank you, Benjie Maxson. You brought God into view and taught me about a different side of Christianity, a side I desperately needed.

Thank you, Mrs. Johnson, for showing me how to communicate well and how to live well.

Thank you, Mr. Beans, for the coaching, for the debates, for the dating advice, and for not giving up on me, even half a world away.

As the world threatens to diminish human connection to cell phones, e-mail, and Facebook comments, I dare you to remind someone how important they are to you, and I dare you to do so face-to-face. Maybe you'll help them hold on a bit longer in a world where we all sometimes feel like giving up.

CHAPTER 53

Last Class

"When you're in over your head, I'll be there with you.
When you're in rough waters, you will not go down. When you're
between a rock and a hard place, it won't be a dead end—
because I am God, your personal God."
—Isaiah 43:2, 3

I'm running out of time with my kids. They know it and I know it. We all deal differently. I'm expecting some to just ignore me, say "Goodbye," and walk out of the gate. Some girls have already admitted they will cry. I will try to be somewhere in the middle between weepy and flippant. Goodbyes are just plain hard for anyone no matter which side you're on. But I assume they are easier if you have no regrets and you've said all you need to say.

Today is one of my last full class periods with my students. I made banana muffins for all 80 students. I think they are enjoying the treat.

I tell them that we have covered all the information, finished all the books, and persevered through grammar lessons and assignments. Then, I tell them that they are about to hear the most important lesson of the year.

I have decided to share with them the most important things I have learned thus far in life. If we aren't constantly sharing what we know, then what's the point? I figure we've been learning from each other all year, but these are the things I will always regret if I don't tell them. So, I do.

"I've been thinking a lot about where you are in your lives and when I was there too. High school wasn't that long ago for me. I have happy memories and I have regrets. I regret that I didn't work harder. I could've gotten better grades. I could've focused a little more in class. I also regret that I cheated."

Ratanak pipes up, "Whoa, Ms. Bo cheats?"

"Cheated. That's past tense. I'm not proud of it. But just so you know, your teachers are smart. They know when you cheat. I know when you cheat.

How do you feel about it? Do you want to graduate knowing you earned it or knowing your friends earned it for you?

"Don't make enemies in school or anywhere. You never know when you will see these people again.

"Appreciate your teachers. They work incredibly hard to help you. Sometimes they don't feel like anyone notices all of their effort. When I was in high school, I wrote many of my teachers a letter thanking them for all they did. I know you all really appreciate your teachers Da Rith and Sokcha. What if you walked up to them and said, 'Hey, I just want to say thank you for helping me this year'? They would be so surprised. Do it!"

I move on to the next subject. "OK, how many of you are dating?"

No one moves.

"Oh, put your hands up! I know some of your girlfriends are over there in ninth grade."

Slowly, a few hands go up.

"I dated one guy in high school. I don't regret it, but I also don't think dating in high school is the best choice. How many times have you been ditched by your friends as soon as they get a girlfriend? And more importantly, you should have your own self-confidence before you involve someone else. Do you understand?

"If you think you are ugly, but you start dating a guy who tells you every day that you are beautiful, you will believe it. But what happens when you break up? Are you still beautiful? Of course you are! But if you didn't believe it before he started telling you, then you are giving him full control of your self-worth. Know who you are before you give your heart to someone else.

"After I graduated high school, I made a list of things that would make the perfect husband..."

"No way! Ms. Bo, you are crazy!" the boys laughed.

"No, I did! Here's why: if you don't know what you are looking for, how will you know when you've found it?"

Vandeth chooses this time to chime in. "Ms. Bo, can I see that list?"

"Ha, ha. No! And until I meet the guy who fulfills everything on that list, or close to it, I'm not wasting my time with him. Never settle!"

"Ms. Bo, what is 'settle'?"

"The word 'settle' is like 'compromise.' Don't give up until you've found the right person for you.

"Boys, don't date a girl who is *only* beautiful! Because, do you know what you'll have in 40 years? Not much. She'll have wrinkles, gray hair, a few extra pounds, and you won't be able to stand her. You need to find a girl who is much more; a girl you will want to be with forever.

"Students, what did you want to be when you were younger?"

I hear all kinds of responses.

"A swimmer!"

"A dancer!"

"Prime minister!"

"OK, I wanted to be a lifeguard, but my ideas have changed since then. Whatever you choose to be, please, please do not pick a job for the money. Pick something you will love doing for the rest of your life. I will never be rich, and that is OK with me because I know what I want. Do what you are passionate about, what you were made to do.

"OK, I have a question. True or false: your life is your fault."

"False. No, true! False, false!" they shout.

"It's true. One of my favorite teachers in high school told me that, and I'll never forget it. There are certain situations beyond your control, such as where you were born or who your parents are, but how you react to life is up to you.

"If you tell me you got a D in algebra because you had a bad teacher, I won't believe you. If you tell me you are bored because your friends are boring, make new friends. If you want a great life, *make* a great life. When you are 80 years old, do not call me and tell me how unhappy you are, because you made most of the decisions in your life that got you there!"

I can see the lightbulbs illuminating, brightening.

"Let's say you forget everything I just said. Don't forget this: you could die today. Wake up every morning and remind yourself of that. What if you walked out of those gates today after school and got hit by a moto? Would you be OK with that?"

"No!" they all yell simultaneously. Smiling back at me and leaning forward about to topple over in their seats, I know they are hearing me. "Yeah, none of us want to die! But if you did, would you have regrets? Did you start a fight with your mom this morning? Did you ignore a friend today who needed someone to talk to? Did a teacher catch you cheating? Have you been ignoring God? Only you know the answers to all those questions. Remind yourself every day that you are not guaranteed tomorrow. How do you want to be remembered?

"So did you get it? Did you capture the most important lesson I've ever taught you? Thank you for being great, great students. You've taught me a lot. I will miss you all."

I give the same basic talk to all three of my classes with a few adjustments based on age and maturity. I could say, "They were probably just listening because they had nothing else to do" or "They were just glad it wasn't English class," but I know better.

They heard me. They were listening because we respect each other. By now, I know their handwriting, how they walk, and who they have crushes on. I know what makes each of them laugh and what hurts them too. I know when they are just looking at me and not really listening. I also know when they are actually learning from me, and today was one of those days.

I confirmed my ticket home. I leave on July 1. That gives me 11 days to learn a few more lessons, have a few more laughs with my kids, and drink a few more glasses of sugarcane juice. I've been taking a lot of pictures of "typical" things, because they really aren't that typical to anyone else. I'm spending extra time with Fay. I'm trying, with difficulty, to remember what life is like at home. I suppose I'll know soon enough.

CHAPTER 54

Forever Foreign

"Not one of these people, even though their lives of faith were exemplary, got their hands on what was promised. God had a better plan for us: that their faith and our faith would come together to make one completed whole, their lives of faith not complete apart from ours."
—*Hebrews 11:39, 40*

I don't want to be in Cambodia. This hurts too much. I feel so horribly alone. I feel empty, useless, pathetic, invisible, and uninteresting. Last night was another rough evening because of this awful eating disorder. I wrote a desperate e-mail to Ben and Ashley as I let out a few sobs that my roommates never heard. I fell asleep between tears. I woke up feeling pretty hopeless.

"I am at the bottom. I have food, oxygen, and water; that's it. I am lacking a stable environment, support, self-respect, and any sort of wholeness or purpose I might've hoped for. I am lacking. I am struggling."

This entry is from my journal on October 2, 2007, the day I broke down at school and couldn't stop crying. I hyperventilated and had a panic attack. It is interesting to read now, because at that point I didn't think it could get much worse, but it did.

That was October. I hadn't started binging and purging in an attempt to feel better, I hadn't been violated by that creep when I was out walking, I hadn't been hit by a car, I hadn't been cursed at by the children on the street.

No surprises here; this has been a painful year. I don't write this from some mountaintop where all clarity has been granted to me. However, I have learned many lessons along the way.

As I look at my eating disorder, I am not proud of the fact that I've taken up binging and purging, but I am not ashamed. This isn't the life I want, and I am not scared to talk about it or admit that I am human just like everyone else. Someday I'll be healed and this pain will be a distant memory.

Yesterday, in desperate need of perspective, I escaped to a bookstore to sit and think. There in the store I promised myself that I would not binge or purge for the next 10 days. This eating disorder has made me its prisoner. On bad days I am not present in my life, I am merely existing in it.

As I prepare to go home, I realize that this could be a stressful time of adjustment. I do not want to slip into the bad habits I have started here and I am determined to leave Cambodia feeling healthy. I am seeking to forgive myself and move on with the lessons I've learned.

Besides close friends and family no one knew about my eating disorder until I arrived overseas. As I have given myself permission to share my struggles and accept my humanity, I've received incredible e-mails from people sharing their own battles.

Once again, it pays to be honest with yourself and those around you. We would never have had those kinds of life-changing conversations unless one of us was willing to start them.

I know that I should be ecstatic to be leaving, but I'm afraid to go home. I fear what I've turned into. Will these habits follow me forever? Will what I have learned here affect me negatively or positively for the rest of my life? I can't answer these questions until I get off the plane. I have no idea what the next few months of my life will be like. I am hopeful, but anxious.

I've been talking to missionaries and reading books about the process of reentry after working in the mission field. There are a lot of horror stories. For some it is easy, for some it takes years. The most repeated information I've heard is that upon reentering your "home" country most people won't be that interested. They think it's cool you went overseas and may ask, "What was the food like?" or "So, did you have fun?" But, they will be satisfied with a few words and will likely not ask anything else.

Coming from a crazy, life-changing, intense experience, this seems like a huge slap in the face. Does anyone care at all? No, they just won't ever get it. And this, I think, will be intensely frustrating. The books don't offer much help. They say, "Just prepare for the fact that your experience can be important to you, even if most people back home don't care."

So, with this information in mind, I've come up with different responses to the question, "So, how was Cambodia?" Because different people will want different answers, I'm trying to prepare for that and not be offended.

Not everyone wants to hear the entire, lengthy story and that's OK.

No number of pictures or stories will ever fully do this experience justice. That's hard to swallow because this has changed my life forever, and no one back home will ever really get it. I don't know if *I* really get it. I imagine it will all feel like a dream, and I will wonder, *Did that really happen? Am I exaggerating? Was it real?*

I'm no fortune-teller, and I don't have the gift of prophecy, so I can't predict the future. Maybe things will be just peachy and I will adjust *no problema*. But I'd rather be ready for the worst so that I don't feel like I've been slapped in the face with the changes and difficulties that are bound to accompany me at home.

Ten days left in Cambodia. Five days of school. Three days of testing. Seventy-one goodbyes. One Sabbath candle. One plane ride. Home.

CHAPTER 55

Fitting

"If we truly knew all the answers in advance as to the meaning of life and the nature of God and the destiny of our souls, our belief would not be a leap of faith and it would not be a courageous act of humanity; it would just be...a prudent insurance policy."
—Elizabeth Gilbert

Hat? *Check.*
Sunglasses? *Check.*
Sunscreen? *Check.*
iPod? *Check.*
Mask? *Check.*
On Sunday mornings I enjoy my weekly bike ride. So 6:35 a.m. finds me leaving the mission and braving the streets yet again. I have never seen another foreigner riding a bike where I do. I'm not sure if I'm naive or just very comfortable. Sometimes I think I am the only non-Cambodian living here. Sometimes I think I am turning into one.

I head south toward the red-light district. I would prefer quieter, less-busy roads, but those don't exist in Phnom Penh, so crazy, never-ending traffic is my only option. I listen to Lenny Kravitz's version of "American Woman," which gives me courage to face the chaos.

I stick to the right side of the road because that is the hip where my iPod is tucked under my shirt, so it is less likely to be grabbed by a passing moto on my left.

I pass women balancing pots full of noodles on their heads, people sitting, men loading trucks, and children playing in the mud. As I breathe harder and harder in the heat of the sun, my face becomes sweaty from the mask covering my nose and mouth. My sunglasses start slipping off my nose as I push them back on. *Pedal, pedal, pedal, deep breath…hack! hack! Ugghhh, no deep breaths!*

Phnom Penh has recently grown fond of roundabouts. The first one I pass has a statue of a revolver handgun in the middle. Apparently, after the war everyone was asked to turn in their guns, and they were melted into this memorial as a symbol of peace. Really, it's just a joke because the statue is *really* puny. If there were no hard feelings and *everyone* turned over their weapons, the statue would be much, much bigger.

I turn right and head toward Wat Phnom, pedaling past markets on my way. Everyone is yelling and buying: chickens (dead and alive), lotus pods, coconuts, soda, and vegetables.

I turn left at Wat Phnom, a bell-shaped statue on a small hill. Apparently this is where the founder of the city, some ancient goddess, is buried. Now monks live there. It is the rainy season, so my legs are splattered and muddy from the water on the road. I glance left and right to avoid getting hit by any cars. If I did get hit, it would be blamed on *me*, and they'd most likely charge *me* money!

Last week JC and I were out on his moto, and he scratched a car with his handlebar. Unfortunately, he didn't scratch *any* car; no, he scratched a gold Lexus with a very angry Khmer government official inside! After at least two hours of arguing, I gave JC the only money I had, $30, and encouraged him to use it so that we could head home.

The man told JC that because he had a rich American wife (me, apparently) he should pay the $200 he felt he deserved to fix the scratch! JC ended up finding someone to fix the small scratch for $1.25, but he was forced to pay the driver and the police officer $100 for their trouble! JC hardly makes that much in a month. It made me sick.

I continue pedaling my way toward the king's palace. Apparently Cambodia has a queen; something I didn't realize until someone told me that today is her birthday. To commemorate the occasion, her picture is posted all over town surrounded by pink flowers and gaudy flashing lights.

I arrive at the riverside. Usually this part of town is thriving with tourists, but at 7:00 a.m. it sits strangely motionless. Well, I have yet to witness "motionlessness" in Cambodia—maybe "less chaotic" would be more appropriate.

The riverside stinks because this is where many people dump their garbage and the oil ships come in. I hold my breath past a few smokers watching me and press on.

My legs begin growing weary, but I know that if I stop, even for a minute, I'll be surrounded by people very quickly. As I turn toward home, I take a few back roads and watch people coming out to set up their shops. A shirtless father stands holding his small daughter. He points at me and waves; I smile and wave back, but then I feel like an idiot because it's not like they can see my smile under my purple face mask.

I don't really know where I am going or what road I am on, but I just sort of follow traffic awhile until I get back to streets I recognize.

I ride past pagodas with monks chanting inside and police officers doing absolutely nothing, which is what they'll do all day. Even now, with only a few days left in Cambodia, I find myself shocked that I am still here experiencing this.

But then I realize that this works for Cambodians. This is all they know. So as much as I struggle to adjust and as frustrating as their culture can be to me, it isn't supposed to fit me. It fits them.

Imagine if someone said to you, "America has serial killers and druggies and prostitutes, so *you* must be a serial killer, druggy, and prostitute!"

That doesn't make any sense, does it? It isn't fair to label or judge someone solely based upon the country they come from. Is it fair to label or judge anyone anyway? As these thoughts run through my mind, I wonder, *What if they don't dislike their lives as much as I assume they should? My country isn't perfect either. The entire country of Cambodia doesn't support prostitution, human trafficking, and corruption. What if they aren't OK with it but they live with it because they have to? I'm not OK with America's problems, yet I am pretty content there.*

As I continue my ride, my thoughts turn spiritual. I'm still struggling to get a grasp on my relationship with God. What I don't understand is how God affects my life today. What is prayer? Is God working differently today than He did 2,000 years ago? I want to make sense of what I've seen. I need help doing it and living with it and learning from it. If God is God, I hope He'll help me.

I believe Cambodia has given God a platform for me to learn from Him without knowing it. How does God use people and experiences? If God had to use Cambodia to teach me about life, I must be pretty stubborn.

I turn onto the street I've called home for almost a year. I pass the creeps playing pool, and I smile at the guard I can't communicate with any other way. I park my rugged, red mountain bike that has loyally carried me through this year. I stretch my legs a bit. *Oh, how this country has changed me.*

CHAPTER 56

Safety, Freedom, and Justice

"We hold these Truths to be self-evident, that all Men are created equal, that they are endowed by their Creator with certain unalienable Rights, that among these are Life, Liberty, and the pursuit of Happiness."
—*Thomas Jefferson*

Right now the students are finishing final exams, taking lots of pictures, and slowly saying their goodbyes. Right now they are the nicest they've been all year, which is fine by me.

While the fear of going home is always fresh in my mind, I'm trying instead to think about all the things I'm looking forward to. In fact, big surprise, I made a list.

First thing I'd like to do upon returning home is to roll in the grass. Then, I'd like to lie on some carpet. Neither of these were things I ever anticipated missing, that is, until I got here. Everything here is dirt and tile. There isn't much that is warm and cozy in Asian homes. They need to be functional, and carpet isn't functional because dirt gets ground in and it stinks if you have animals. But with tile they just hose it down and it's clean. So, I understand the rationale, but I still really miss comfortable things like carpeting.

The second thing I am eagerly awaiting is winter—a change in climate, cold weather, snow. More than just the cooler weather though, I am looking forward to the need for warm, cuddly things like a big blanket, slippers, a cup of hot cocoa, or a bowl of soup. There is just no need for warm and cuddly things in Cambodia. I don't want to touch people; we are all so hot and sticky.

When it is even mildly cold, my kids will come with jackets. They don't really need them, but they never get to use them. So when the sun is behind a cloud, the jackets come out. I see girls wearing turtleneck sweaters. Why? Because they want to look like the models they've seen on TV.

A stall at Toul Tom Poung market sells ridiculously cheap North Face jackets. I wonder how they stay in business. The average temperature here is 90 degrees. So, upon landing in Colorado, I want to curl up in a blanket with a book and a cup of tea and just relax.

OK, so after I roll in the grass and put on my slippers, I'd really like to get some Mexican food: Taco Bell, Casa Bonita, or Three Margaritas; I'm not picky. Asia is getting more and more daring with branching out past rice, but Mexican food just hasn't caught on.

I'm looking forward to safety, freedom, and justice. This may sound so cheesy, but until you've lived without them you just might not appreciate them. I hate, *hate* being outside here. I never feel safe. I don't feel like I am protected by anyone or any law. I miss the freedom of feeling protected and having rights as a human being, much less a woman. And along with that, I miss the feeling of knowing that if something were to happen to me at the hands of another, they would be punished.

Whatever you believe of America is fine. I know we've got our problems. But they are few compared to the corruption that seeps into the most innocent of this country. I am supremely excited for the day when I can walk down the street and be completely ignored, when people look right past me like I don't even exist. I am tired of feeling like the main event at a freak show.

Last, I can't wait for the moment when I am in a room surrounded by people and all of them are speaking a language I understand, can relate to, and can hold a conversation in. Here, I can be surrounded by 30 kids or a few dozen adults, and I feel excluded. I am rarely a part of conversations or jokes. I am always the one saying, "Huh? What did he say?"

It especially stinks to hear a Khmer conversation that goes, "Blah, blah, blah, blah, Ms. Bo, blah, blah, blah!" The worst is to hear my name among Khmer curse words. Those are the times I pretend I don't know those words, smile, and walk away. I want to be able to use words with people.

I want to feel understood. I want to understand.

I'm looking forward to that.

CHAPTER 57

Sprung a Leak

"You must be the change you wish to see in the world."
—*Mahatma Gandhi*

I'm sick again. Ridiculous. I had an awful flu back in January, and I've had monthly colds all year. My oversanitized upbringing in the States has left me defenseless against the infestation of germs in Cambodia.

This week of testing has been slow and boring. I hand out the tests, then sit, watch, grade papers, walk around every few minutes, and calculate more grades.

Today is yet another day of testing. I am working up in the library while my kids are in the classroom at study hall. I haven't been feeling that great all morning. I feel like I need to throw up, but I can't. Suddenly, feeling the urge, I scurry toward the bathroom, but I nearly collapse as the concrete in front of me spins. Looking up, black spots appear and I pass out. Sweating and breathing hard, I come to and sit awhile, listening to the giggles and screams of second graders running around.

I feel stronger after a few minutes, so I return to my spot in the library. I fall asleep for a few minutes while Fay putters around. All too soon I have to go back to class. I am OK in class, but again, later in the afternoon, I am dizzy, so I lie down. I can hardly sit up when the school day ends, so I opt to leave my bike at school and catch a ride home with Fay.

It feels like I have sprung a leak somewhere and the blood is slowly draining out of my body. Any energy I do have is being sucked right out of me. At home I eat with Fay and then head to my room. My whole body is aching, and I am so weak I can do little else but lie around. I throw up and crawl in bed at about 5:30 p.m.

I wake up the next morning and decide to stay home. I don't want to miss the last day of school, which is tomorrow. As I lie in bed, I think, *People used to die from the flu. What if I died of the flu four days before I was going to go home?*

I turn away from my sobering thoughts and think about my conversation yesterday with my eighth graders. They were telling me about the fear they have living here. This is the first time I'd heard them talk like this. A few of them have seen people get stabbed while riding past on a moto. They've seen kids getting beat up. They've seen gangs with knives on the hunt for their next victim. Last week a Khmer teacher at a government school was stabbed to death by some of his students. My kids have all had run-ins with what they call the "gangsters" in Phnom Penh. If you dress nicer than them, if you dress worse than them, if you look at them, if you don't look at them, you are always at risk, always in fear.

So I said, "What can you do to be safe? Is there any way to avoid them?"

"Anything makes them mad. No way to be safe."

They are scared. I am scared.

I asked them, "Do you think Cambodia will always be a scary place for you to live?"

"I think Prime Minister Hun Sen will change Cambodia and everything will get better," Joanna said as she looked intensely at the ground.

I don't believe what she said, and I don't think she does either. I wasn't about to contradict her though. I think the hope that things will improve is all my kids have to hold on to. I can't take that away from them.

The facts about Cambodia are sad enough, but leaving my kids here is even harder. I worry that my girls will be mistreated and abused like many of the other Khmer women. I worry that my boys will get into drugs because I know some of them already are. I've talked to several of the high school students about drinking; I'm not sure they hear me. I'm scared that my kids won't see all the great things I see in them and that they'll give up, settle, or compromise. I'm afraid that they'll forget how wonderful and talented they are, so they'll become absorbed in the prostitution, drugs, or worse that surrounds them.

I can't rescue them. I can't protect them from everything. But their entire culture is working against them, and I feel it is stronger than my one year of service could ever save them from. I fear they'll look back on our year together and the memories will slowly fade.

As much as I tried to help them feel important, loved, valued, and appreciated, how far does that really go? I can hope for the best. I know that for the rest of my life anytime I hear the word "Cambodia" these kids will come to mind, and I'll wonder, *Are they OK? Are they successful businessmen or druggies on the street? Are they teachers, preachers, and doctors like they wanted to become, or did they give up on their dreams and become what they never wanted to be?*

I wonder if I will ever have answers to these questions. Probably not. If I could answer all these questions now, I'd stop asking, learning, growing, and trying to make a difference. It is when we lose our sense of wonder and questioning that we lose our love of life too. If I knew for sure what the lives of my students held, I'd find it easy to forget about them and move on. I'd be more likely to forget all that I've learned. But I will forever feel that urge to keep in touch and pray for them.

I have often felt hopeless here, but I suppose if I had no hope at all, I wouldn't have lasted the year. It is in the hope that my kids will indeed someday "be the change" that this country needs that has given me strength to stay.

CHAPTER 58

For the Last Time

"You will either step forward into growth or you will step back into safety."
—*Abraham Maslow*

I still feel sick and weak, but it is the last day of school and the last time I'll see most of my kids.

As soon as I arrive at school, all of the teachers say, "Ughh, you look horrible! You should go home and rest."

"Thank you. I'll be all right," I say and trudge on through the day. My kids definitely notice I am not my bubbly self.

The last day at CAS is just partying and games anyway. So, I set them loose, and they are happy. By mid-morning I am dizzy, so I make my way to the library where I fall asleep. When I wake up, there are a few notes and cards scattered around me on the beanbag. School is out. My kids are gone.

I didn't really get to say goodbye to each individual, but really, we've been saying goodbye for several months now. Maybe this is just easier.

I clean out my desk, thinking about how many times I've opened and closed these drawers. Surveying the room for remains of my students, a pencil, a notebook, or a shoe, I see nothing. Walking toward the door, almost sentimental, but still thrilled to be going home, I'm grateful for what I've learned here. I catch a ride with Fay, get home, and sleep for five hours. I arouse long enough to assure Tim and Fay I'm alive then go back to bed.

I wake up on Sabbath morning, wanting to go to church, but I can't make it. I sleep for six hours straight, getting up only to vomit. Then it is nighttime, so I go back to sleep, again.

Sunday morning is graduation. I really want to go because any of the kids I missed on Friday will be there. I drag myself to school and am eagerly greeted by my eleventh-grade girls. We sit through most of the service until concerned Sayanet says, "Ms. Bo, let's go."

She doesn't even ask. She takes me by the arm, gets me a pillow, and acts as my personal fan as I fall asleep on top of a wooden picnic table. After awhile, I know my presence at graduation is quite pointless, so I get a ride home. Upon arriving, I fall asleep for four hours.

Fay comes in later. "All right dear, we are taking you to the hospital. I cannot send you home this way. Your parents will be so scared if you come home sick as a dog!"

She's probably right; I have not been doing well at all. But I am really stubborn, and I don't care for hospitals. Plus, hospitals are different in Cambodia, and I'd rather lie in bed suffering than have someone stabbing me with dirty needles, unable to explain what they're doing. She convinces me to go because there is a new hospital nearby that looks reliable, and she's afraid what my parents will say if she sends me home this way.

The Ratanak Royal Hospital is clean, they speak some English, and I feel confident here. I describe my symptoms. They take my vitals. They do a blood test. I have a low white blood cell count, so apparently that shows a viral infection.

The doctor tells me that all of the pills I am currently taking are outdated and probably doing me no good. He gives me some simple electrolyte packets, nausea/vomiting pills, and Tylenol.

I am so bummed I had to get some "viral infection" the last weekend I am here. I missed out on quite a bit. My girls wanted to hang out; I couldn't. The teachers got together for lunch; I couldn't. And I suddenly find myself craving really greasy food I know I can't eat and wouldn't normally eat anyway, just to add to the frustration.

The goodbyes were not what I had hoped for, but I told my kids everything I wanted them to know. I have no regrets.

I'm living on 7-Up and ramen noodles, when they stay down, and thinking about tragically dying my last few days in Cambodia. It doesn't help when Fay is joking about it too. "Wouldn't it be sad if we had to call Heather's parents and tell them that Cambodia finally killed her?"

Fortunately, it is Monday, June 30, 2008, and I am going home tomorrow. The pain isn't so bad today. I am finishing my packing and laundry, and tonight I'm going out for dinner or watching a few friends eat dinner. Either way, these are my last goodbyes.

Tomorrow morning, I'm walking out the door and braving the streets for the last time, locking up my bike for the last time, driving past the school for the last time, haggling with Khmers for the last time. I'm leaving Cambodia.

Really, what was I thinking coming to Cambodia? I had no idea what I was going to face. I guess it is that "ignorance-is-bliss" factor that gets us to do almost anything. Sorting through all the mail I've received since I've been here, I marvel at how effortlessly it seems to arrive—a lot less bumpy than my own journey.

Home is within sight. I realize that I still have a lot to learn, but I'm ready to continue the journey.

CHAPTER 59

Landing

"Praise the bridge that carried you over."
—*George Colman*

I hate goodbyes!" says Fay through watery eyes. "Can we just do this quickly?"

"Sounds good to me," I say. "You know how much I love you both. We'll see each other again someday. Travel safe."

Fay wraps me in a big hug, just like she did when I first met her at the airport 10 months earlier. The hug is the same, just as warm, just as genuine, yet so much has changed.

Now, I am stronger. Now, I have seen, felt, experienced, and grown more than I could ever measure. I have taught. I have traveled to places I never thought I'd see. I've been stretched and pulled, challenged and tested. Since that first day in Cambodia, much has changed, some good and some bad, but I made it.

Fay and Tim load up the luggage they'll need on their two-month furlough. They are so brave for doing this year after year. Fay waves out the back window until I can't see her anymore.

The next morning it is time to catch my flight. I have been packing for about a month now, so not much is left to be done.

A few of my students were persistent in asking to take me to the airport. I really didn't want to prolong the goodbye process, but they insisted.

I need to leave home at 8:30 a.m. for the airport.

Leckanah said, "We'll be over to help at 6:30."

"Umm, no you won't! I'll still be sleeping! How about 8?"

The doorbell rings at 7:20 a.m. It is Phalkun, "Good morning, Ms. Bo! I know you said not come until 8, but I been sitting outside since 7 and so bored!"

"Come on in."

She helps me weigh my bags. Soon, a few other girls show up. I'm dreading this goodbye.

We pack up and drive to the airport. We talk a lot about the future.

"What if we don't graduate high school? Will you get marry soon? Will you miss us?" they ask.

I offer only what I can, "Girls, I don't know the future, but you are all bright and funny and wonderful. You'll be OK. I will e-mail you as soon as I get home. You are a part of my life now. I won't forget you."

They walk me to the gate with the saddest puppy eyes I've ever seen. No one really says anything as I try to figure out how dramatically my life is about to change, again.

We make the dreaded goodbyes. I cry, of course. But it is a lot easier knowing that I am going home.

Twenty-six hours later, I am flying over Denver, Colorado. The pilot comes on, "Ladies and gentleman, please fasten your seatbelts and return your seats to their..." His voice trails off as I reflect on the last time I was in this exact location a year ago.

Gripping the armrests with eyes closed tightly. *Breathe in, breathe out.* I've come full circle. I'm back where I started, but not really.

Inching closer and closer toward the earth, the wheels finally make contact. As soon as they touch the ground, tears flood my eyes. An overwhelming sense of relief sweeps over me: this is home.

Flashing through my head are all the things I've seen and experienced: the pain, exhaustion, shock, and disbelief. Also, the smiles, jokes, side-splitting laughter, and hugs.

The reality hits me that things are going to change, things have changed. I survived Cambodia and will continue life, never forgetting this experience as long as I live.

Tears continue flowing down my cheeks as I realize, I cannot deny that as bumpy as it has been and as many questions as I've had about God, *something* brought me safely home. *Something.*

I've sought control of my life in many ways, but the realization that I have no idea how I just survived the last year brings me to a quiet respect for this moment. Right here, right now, I have no words, no explanations as to how

I am alive and breathing. I can't account for my safety and protection. I can't take credit for my safe travels all over the world.

My own smallness overwhelms me as I stand up in disbelief, humbled.

Like the end of an intriguing movie, I am still trying to fully understand it. Unable to answer these questions, I'm left with a sense of awe.

I whisper a quiet "thank you" to whomever or whatever is responsible, because I'm aware, for the first time, it isn't me.

I gather my bags, walk off the plane, and keep living.

EPILOGUE

"Life isn't about finding yourself. Life is about creating yourself."
—*George Bernard Shaw*

Hey, how was Africa?" she asks me excitedly.

"Well, I don't know. I actually went to Cambodia," I answer.

"Oh yeah, whatever. Cambodia. So, was it fun?"

"Parts of it were fun. Mostly, it was the hardest, most life-changing year of my life."

The pasted smile fades from her face and her eyes focus intently on me, "Oh, really? Wow. Tell me about it."

Now we're talking.

My year in Cambodia was amazing, but I am not quick to forget that it was amazingly hard. I don't want to forget so quickly. Only in our pain, our stories, and our honesty do we truly learn from one another lessons we'll never forget.

That's why I wrote this book. Maybe this book can be fuel for your own journey. We all struggle. We all hurt. It's up to us to learn something from our journey. No one can force life's lessons on me. I can complain in saying, "This is what Cambodia did to *me*." Or I can be grateful in recognizing, "This is what Cambodia taught me."

Landing back in the States brought peace to my soul. Hugging my family, talking with good friends, sharing my stories, and moving on with life has been the purest source of healing. I'm moving on *with* all my experiences, not in spite of them.

Soon after returning home, I started seeing a trauma counselor to work through my Cambodia experiences and a dietician for my bulimia. For several weeks nightmares haunted me. Healing is no quick fix. So I surrounded myself with supportive people who have been helping me find my way back home, wherever that turns out to be.

Along with mental and emotional healing came physical healing. A pantry of bugs seems to have hitchhiked their way home with me, including, but not limited to: worms, giardia, parasites, yeast, bacteria, and amoebas. *Oh joy.*

Fall semester finds me back at good ol' Union College. Reentry to the college life has been bumpy, yet absolutely necessary. And guess what? While I swore I'd *never* be a teacher, my major is now secondary education. Someday I'll be right back in a high school classroom teaching English. I'll never forget how I ended up there.

Would I do it all over again? Of course not! I wouldn't do it over again, especially not the same way, but I am glad it happened—and grateful to be on this side of it.

Back in the arms of familiarity, family, and friends I still seek answers to those questions that arose overseas. In Cambodia, when I was still talking to God, I prayed three big prayer requests. I begged God to help me leave the eating disorder in Cambodia. I prayed for a friend or some kind of nourishing community. I prayed for purpose, some reason He wanted me there.

It wasn't until I began putting this book together that I realized, maybe my prayers were answered.

Since I've been back in the States, binging and purging have almost disappeared. Some days I hardly think about food or dieting or exercise. Those days are huge victories, especially when compared to where I've been. I'm discovering who I really am and who I can be.

I'm not healed completely, but I'm on my way. If God is bigger than the universe, can I really expect Him to be my puppet and adhere to my timeline? Do I really want to serve a God that would?

Loneliness was a horrible part of living in Cambodia. But between Tim, Fay, and Polly I made it through. They remain close friends and probably always will be. I never once stopped to consider the possibility that God could use people to reach me. That seemed too easy, too obvious. I now realize that these amazing people were an answer to prayer, whether or not I chose to call them that. Now I do.

Finally, I begged God to show me a purpose of why I was placed in Cambodia. Why, why, why? I just couldn't see it while I was there.

Back in college, sitting in a psychology class with 26 other students, I realize that I made a difference in Cambodia. I feel like anything I do here pales when compared to what I've done. I see that I mattered, that someone had to teach those kids, and it was I.

Each week my inbox is flooded with e-mails from my students in Cambodia, the same students who joked, "Ms. Bo, when you write a book, can we get your autograph?" I miss them.

My bitterness and anger toward a God who never came through for me is slowly ceasing. God has yet to write "Here I am, Heather" in the sky or send lightning from heaven at my request, but I believe that He exists. I can't prove God, but I can't disprove Him either.

I believe in God because I'm still alive and there's no good reason why.

I believe in God because somehow blood keeps pumping through my capillaries and my lungs inhale and exhale.

I believe in God because beautiful people continue coming into my life, blessing and teaching me daily.

I believe in God because I believe in evil. I don't doubt the awful events that take place in life. There must be its opposite. There must be good. There must be healing out there somewhere.

I believe in God because there are too many things in life I just can't explain. That is God. God is the bigness of life, and I'm humbled by it.

I still have my questions. I still have my doubts. But I'm learning to learn. I can take this a day at a time—that's really all I can do. I'm learning that maybe I'm enough and I'm worth loving.

I haven't found God. I'm *finding* God.

If it took 10 months in Cambodia to get me to this point, I can say, yes, it *was* a struggle—but honestly, it was all worth it.

Surprising Things Happen When You

Follow God

When God called Curt DeWitt to be a missionary in Africa, Curt found himself fighting off spitting cobras, helping capture criminals, and spiritually wrestling with the powers of darkness. In this hilarious account of his African adventures Curt proves that ending up where you least expected can be more exciting and satisfying than you ever imagined.

Paperback, 156 pages.
978-0-8280-1942-2.

Books That Feed Your Mind, Heart, and Soul

Hunger
Discover how you can truly encounter God through such spiritual practices as simplicity, solitude, worship, community, and fasting. With fresh insight and practical guidance Jon Dybdahl leads you on a journey that will satisfy the longing of your soul. 978-0-8127-0458-7.

Miracles, Faith, and Unanswered Prayers
Why does God answer some prayers and not others? Why do some people seem to experience miracles, while others don't? Does God play favorites? Richard Jensen tackles some of life's thorny questions in this straight-forward exploration of Christian faith—and what it is not. 978-0-8280-2015-2.

Majesty
Worship is a vibrant, ongoing, authentic encounter with God—a life-changing experienc In these pages Joseph Kidder shares scriptura principles to guide you into a genuine worship experience that will transform your soul an leave you hungry for God's presence. 978-0-8280-2423-5.

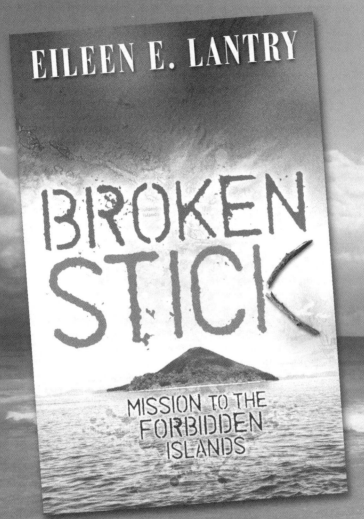

The missionary wasn't afraid to die . . .

EILEEN E. LANTRY

BROKEN STICK

MISSION TO THE FORBIDDEN ISLANDS

. . . and he wasn't leaving the island.

Norman Ferris stood his ground as the warriors thundered across the sacred beach toward him. He had come to this remote island to tell the devil worshippers about the one true God . . . and he wasn't leaving until he did so. 978-0-8280-2069-5

BOOKS TO ENRICH YOUR RELATIONSHIP WITH JESUS

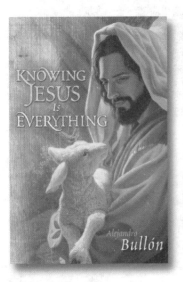

Knowing Jesus Is Everything

The Christian life is too difficult—if you don't know Jesus personally. No matter what you do (or don't do), you don't stand a chance without Him. Alejandro Bullón offers guidance for pursuing a genuine friendship with Jesus. 978-0-8280-2381-8

Savior

You've read the greatest story ever told—but never quite like this. Written in modern language without the disjointed interruption of chapter or verse, Jack Blanco merges the four Gospel accounts into one fresh, unified narrative. This is the timeless, captivating story of Jesus, our Savior. 978-0-8127-0469-3

Revelation's Great Love Story

Larry Lichtenwalter explores the final book of the Bible and unveils a side of Revelation that is seldom portrayed: Christ's passionate love for humanity. Open your eyes to the extraordinary love of our Savior for His rebellious, undeserving children—and the incredible reasons we can love Him in return. 978-0-8127-0460-0